SEO 201

Learn Search Engine Optimization
With Smart Internet Marketing Strategies
Expanded & Updated

Adam Clarke

Digital Book Guru, Publisher.
Cover Design: Digital Book Guru.
Production and Composition: Digital Book Guru.

Adam Clarke has completed a certificate in the Google Analytics Qualified Individual & Google AdWords Qualified Individual programs.

SEO 2016: Learn search engine optimization with smart internet marketing strategies.
Adam Clarke
Kindle ASIN B00NH0XZR0
Print ISBN-10: 151534567X
Print ISBN-13: 978-1515345671

Table of contents.

- Simple link building strategies.
- Advanced link building strategies.

Preface to the updated edition.

It didn't take long for this book to become a best seller on search engine optimization after its original publication in 2013.

The success of this book can only be attributed to its focus on making a powerful but difficult skillset easy to understand.

Now this book has been expanded and updated to cover how SEO works now and likely in the near future. All of the resources and tools have been updated and made relevant for 2015 and 2016. It has been updated to include broader coverage of the basics, and filled with more techniques for advanced users. And due to requests by readers, it has been loaded with more helpful tools and resources, so you can save time and get bigger results.

If you are a beginner, there is a small amount of technical information included in this book. If you really want to learn search engine optimization this cannot be avoided. We've made these areas as simple as possible, while providing additional tools and resources that will make it easy to speed up your journey to SEO mastery.

If you are an advanced SEO optimization professional, this book covers updated summaries of Google's latest updates, updated summaries of SEO marketing best practices to refresh your memory, solutions for common technical problems, and new tools and resources to sharpen your skillset—all written in an easy-to-read format, so refreshing your knowledge doesn't feel like a chore.

If you have requests for future updates, please contact me with my details at the end of this book and I'll be happy to take on board your suggestions.

Introduction.

So you've picked up SEO 2016 and decided to learn search engine optimization. Congratulations. SEO marketing has changed my life and it can change yours.

Over 10-years ago, I achieved my first number one ranking in Google for my family's accounting business. The phone started ringing with new customers every day. I was hooked.

Since then, I have used search engine optimization to grow small family-owned businesses, sex toy stores, large international fashion brands, and hotel chains. One thing never ceases to amaze me — the power of SEO as an Internet marketing tool for growing any business. I have grown small businesses into giant companies in just one or two years — simply from working the client's site up to the top position in Google.

Unfortunately, learning how to use SEO is difficult, if not impossible, for most business owners, Internet marketers and even tech-heads.

I have a theory on why this is so...

Sifting through the amount of information flooding the Internet about SEO is overwhelming. In many cases, the advice published is outdated or misleading.

And the constant updates by Google make it hard for SEO beginners and gurus alike to keep up with what works.

SEO can be simple and used by absolutely anyone to rank at the top of Google, grow their business and make money online.

It's a matter of having up-to-date information on how Google works, using effective techniques and taking action.

Whether you're a complete SEO newbie or well-versed Internet marketing veteran, SEO 2016 covers these areas and makes it as simple as possible to achieve rankings, traffic and sales.

Enjoy.

Introduction to how Google works.

You can feel like a dog chasing its own tail trying to figure out how Google works.

There are thousands of bloggers and journalists spreading volumes of information that simply isn't true. If you followed all the advice about SEO written on blogs, it's unlikely you would receive top listings in Google, and there's a risk you could damage your site performance and make it difficult to rank at all.

Let me tell you a secret about bloggers…

Articles about the latest SEO updates, techniques or tips are often written by interns, assistants, or even ghostwriters. Their job is to write articles. The majority of blog posts about SEO are rarely written by experts or professionals with the day-to-day responsibility of growing site traffic and achieving top rankings in search engines.

Can you learn from someone who doesn't even know how to do it themselves?

You can't. This is why you have to take the advice spread by blog posts with a grain of salt.

Don't get me wrong. I love bloggers. There are bloggers out there who practice and blog about SEO, and do it well. But it has become increasingly difficult to sort the wheat from the chaff.

Fear not. This chapter will disperse common misconceptions about SEO, show you how to avoid falling into Google's bad books and reveal how to stay up-to-date with how Google ranks sites.

But first, to understand how Google works today, we must understand a little bit about Google's history.

Old-school methods that no longer work.

In the early days of Google — over 15 years ago — Google started a smarter search engine and a better experience for navigating the World Wide Web. Google delivered on this promise by delivering relevant search engine results.

Internet users discovered they could simply type what they were looking for into Google — and BINGO — users would find what they needed in the top results, instead of having to dig through hundreds of pages. Google's user base grew fast.

It didn't take long for smart and entrepreneurially minded webmasters to catch on to sneaky little hacks for ranking high in Google.

Webmasters discovered by cramming many keywords into the page, they could get their site ranking high for almost any word or phrase. It quickly spiraled into a competition of who could jam the most keywords into the page. The page with the most repeated keywords won, and rose swiftly to the top of the search results.

Naturally, more and more spammers caught on and Google's promise as the 'most relevant search engine' was challenged. Webmasters and spammers became more sophisticated and found tricky ways of repeating keywords on the page and then completely hiding them from human eyes.

All of a sudden, grandma looking for 'holidays in Florida' would be left with the nasty surprise of arriving at a site about Viagra Viagra Viagra!

How could Google keep its status as the most relevant search engine, if people kept on spamming the results with gazillions of spammy pages, burying the relevant results to the bottom?

Enter the first Google update. Google released a widespread update in November 2003 codenamed 'Florida', effectively stopping spammers in their tracks. This update leveled the playing field by rendering keyword stuffing completely useless and effectively restored balance to the force.

And so began the long history of Google updates — making it hard for spammers to game the system and making ranking high a little more complicated for everyone.

Recent Google updates and how to survive them.

Fast-forward 15 years and ranking in Google has become extremely competitive and considerably more complex.

Simply put, everybody wants to be in Google. Google is fighting to keep its search engine relevant and must constantly evolve to continue delivering relevant results to users.

This hasn't been without its challenges. Just like keyword stuffing, webmasters eventually clued onto another way of gaming the system by having the most 'anchor text' pointing to the page.

If you are not familiar with this term, anchor text is the text contained in external links pointing to a page.

This created another loophole exploited by spammers. In many cases, well-meaning marketers and business owners used this tactic to achieve high rankings in the search results.

Along came a new Google update in 2012, this time called 'Penguin'. Google's Penguin update punished sites with suspicious amounts of links with exact-matched anchor text pointing to a page, by completely delisting sites from the search results. Many businesses that relied on search engine traffic lost all of their sales literally overnight, just because Google believed sites with hundreds of links containing just one phrase didn't acquire those links naturally. Google believed this was a solid indicator the site owner could be gaming the system.

If you find these changes alarming, don't. How to recover from these changes, or to prevent being penalized by new updates, is covered in later chapters. In the short history of Google's major updates, we can discover two powerful lessons for achieving top rankings in Google and staying there.

1. If you want to stay at the top of Google, never rely on one tactic.

2. Always ensure your search engine strategies rely on SEO best practices.

Authority, trust & relevance. Three powerful SEO strategies explained.

Google has evolved considerably from its humble origins in 1993.

Eric Schmidt, former CEO of Google, once reported that Google considered over 200 factors to determine which sites rank higher in the results.

Today, Google has well over 200 factors. Google assesses how many links are pointing to your site, how trustworthy these linking sites are, how many social mentions your brand has, how relevant your page is, how old your site is, how fast your site loads... and the list goes on.

Does this mean it's impossible or difficult to get top rankings in Google?

Nope. In fact, you can have the advantage.

Google's algorithm is complex, but you don't have to be a rocket scientist to understand how it works. In fact, it can be ridiculously simple if you remember just three principles. With these three principles you can determine why one site ranks higher than another, or discover what you have to do to push your site higher than a competitor. These three principles summarize what Google are focusing on in their algorithm now, and are the most powerful strategies SEO professionals are using to their advantage to gain rankings.

The three key principles are: Trust, Authority and Relevance.

1. Trust.

Trust is at the very core of Google's major changes and updates the past several years. Google wants to keep poor-quality, shoddy sites out of the search results, and keep high-quality, legit sites at the top. If your site has high-quality content and backlinks from reputable sources, your site is more likely to be considered a trustworthy source, and more likely to rank higher in the search results.

2. Authority

Previously the most popular SEO strategy, authority is still powerful, but now best used in tandem with the other two principles. Authority is your site's overall strength in your market. Authority is almost a pure numbers game, for example: if your site has one thousand social media followers and backlinks, and your competitors only have fifty social media followers and backlinks, you're probably going to rank higher.

3. Relevance.

Google looks at the contextual relevance of a site and rewards relevant sites with higher rankings. This levels the playing field a bit, and might explain why a niche site or local business can often rank higher than a Wikipedia article. You can use this to your advantage by bulking out the content of your site with relevant content, and use the on-page SEO techniques described in later chapters to give Google a 'nudge' to see that your site is relevant to your market. You can rank higher with less links by focusing on building links from relevant sites. Increasing relevance like this is a powerful strategy and can lead to a high rankings in competitive areas.

How Google ranks sites now — Google's top-10 ranking factors revealed.

You may have wondered if you can find out the exact factors Google uses in their algorithm.

Fortunately, there are a handful of industry leaders who have figured it out, and regularly publish their findings on the Internet. With these publications you can get a working knowledge of what factors Google use to rank sites. These surveys are typically updated every second year, but these factors don't change often, so you can use them to your advantage by knowing which areas to focus on.

A short list of some of the strongest factors contributing to high search rankings:

- Word count.
- Relevant keywords on page.
- Responsive design.
- User signals (click-through-rate, time-on-site, bounce-rate).
- Domain SEO visibility (how strong the domain is in terms of links and authority).
- Site speed.
- Referring domains (number of sites linking to your site).
- Keyword in internal links.
- Content readability.
- Number of images.

If your competitors' pages have more of the above than yours, then it's likely they are going to rank higher. If your pages have more of the above than competitors, then it is likely you will beat them.

Combine this with an understanding of the recent Google updates covered in later sections, and you will know what it takes to achieve top rankings.

The above factors are from the Search Metrics Google Ranking Factors study released in July, 2015. The Search Metrics study is an in-depth look at the high-ranking factors in Google. If you want a deeper look, you can browse the full report by visiting the link below.

Search Metrics: Google Ranking Factors US

http://www.searchmetrics.com/en/knowledge-base/ranking-factors/

Another well-known authority on the SEO industry, called MOZ (previously SEOMOZ), release a survey every two years, combining survey data from world-leading SEOs, and a very detailed analysis of how Google functions today. MOZ also publish this information for free on their site.

MOZ Ranking Factors Survey
http://moz.com/search-ranking-factors

How to stay ahead of Google's updates.

Every now and then, Google releases a significant update to their algorithm, which can have a massive impact on businesses from any industry. To hone your SEO chops and make sure your site doesn't fall into Google's bad books, it's important to stay up-to-date with Google's updates as they are released.

Fortunately, almost every time a major update is released, those updates are reported on by the entire SEO community and often publicly discussed and confirmed by Google staff.

A long extended history of Google's updates would fill this entire book, but with the resources below, you can stay abreast of new Google updates as they are rolled out. This is essential knowledge for anyone practicing SEO, at a beginner or an advanced level.

You can even keep your ear to the ground with these sources and sometimes be forewarned of future updates.

Google Updates by Search Engine Round Table
http://www.seroundtable.com/category/google-updates

Search Engine Round Table is one of the industry's leading blogs on SEO. At the page above, you can browse all of the latest articles on Google updates by a leading authority.

Moz Blog
https://moz.com/blog

The Moz blog is mentioned several times in this book and for good reason — it's pretty much the leading authority blog on all things SEO, and if there's an impending update Google have hinted at, you can catch wind of it here.

Keyword research. The most important step of SEO.

Why is keyword research so important?

Keyword research is the first and most important stage of every SEO project.

Keyword research is the most important stage for two main reasons:

1. If you rank your site highly for the wrong keywords, you can end up spending lots of time and effort, only to discover the keyword you have targeted doesn't receive any traffic.

2. If you haven't investigated the competitiveness of your keywords, you can end up investing lots of time and effort into a particular keyword, only to find it is far too competitive to rank, even on the first page.

These two pitfalls are often the ultimate decider on how successful any SEO project is.

This chapter will cover how to avoid these pitfalls and how to find the best keywords. First, we must define what a keyword is.

What exactly is a keyword?

If you are an SEO newbie, you may be wondering – what is a keyword?

A keyword is any phrase you would like your site to rank for in Google's search results. A keyword can be a single word, or a keyword can also be a combination of words. If you are trying to target a single word, lookout! You will have your work cut out for you. Single word keywords are extremely competitive, and difficult to rank highly for in the search results.

Here's some different kinds of keywords:

Head-term keywords: keywords with one to two words, i.e. classic movies.

Long-tail keywords: keywords with three or more phrases, i.e. classic Akira Kurosawa movies

Navigational keyword: keywords used to locate a particular brand or website. Examples would be Facebook, YouTube or Gmail.

Informational keyword: keywords used to discover on a particular topic. This includes keywords beginning with 'how to…' or 'what are the best..'

Transactional keyword: keywords entered into Google by customers wanting to complete a commercial action, i.e. 'buy jackets online'.

In most cases, targeting head term or navigational keywords for other brands is competitive and not worth the time or effort. Despite their high traffic numbers, they will generally not lead to any sales. On the other hand, long-tail, informational and transactional keywords are good keywords for most SEO projects. They will lead to more customers.

How to generate a massive list of keywords.

There are many ways to skin a cat. The same is true for finding the right keywords.

Before you can find keywords with loads of traffic in Google, you must first develop a list of potential keywords relevant to your business.

Relevance is vital.

If you spend your time trying to cast too wide a net, you can end up targeting keywords irrelevant to your audience.

For example, if you are an online football jacket retailer in the United States, examples of relevant keywords might be:

Buy football jackets
Buy football jackets online
Online football jackets store USA

Irrelevant keywords might be:

Football jacket photos
How to make your own football jacket
Football jacket manufacturers
How to design a football jacket

You can see how the first pool of keywords are more relevant to the target audience of football jacket retailer, and the second pool of keywords are related but unlikely to lead to customers.

Keeping relevance in mind, you must develop a list of potential keyword combinations to use as a resource, so you can then go and uncover the best keywords with a decent amount of traffic each month in Google.

Listed below are powerful strategies you can use to help with generating this list.

1. Steal keywords from competitors.

If you're feeling sneaky, you can let your competitors do the heavy lifting for you and snatch up keywords from their sites.

There are many tools out there created for this sole purpose. A simple tool is the SEOBook keyword analyzer. If you enter a page into this tool within seconds it will scrape a list of the keywords your competitor is targeting on their page. You can then use this to bulk out your keyword list.

SEOBook Keyword Analyzer
http://tools.seobook.com/general/keyword-density/

2. Brainstorm your own master list.

Assuming competitors have been thorough with their research isn't always the best strategy. By brainstorming combinations of keywords, you can generate a giant list of potential keywords.

To do this, sketch out a grid of words your target customer might use. Split the words into different prefixes and suffixes. Next up, combine them into one giant list using the free Mergewords tool. With this strategy you can quickly and easily build up a massive list of relevant keywords.

Mergewords
http://www.mergewords.com

Prefix
- buy
- where do I buy

Middle word
- NFL jerseys

- NFL uniforms
- NFL jackets

Suffixes
- online

Combined keywords
- NFL jerseys
- NFL jerseys online
- NFL uniforms
- NFL uniforms online
- NFL jackets
- NFL jackets online
- buy NFL jerseys
- buy NFL jerseys online
- buy NFL uniforms
- buy NFL uniforms online
- buy NFL jackets
- buy NFL jackets online
- where do I buy NFL jerseys
- where do I buy NFL jerseys online
- where do I buy NFL uniforms
- where do I buy NFL uniforms online
- where do I buy NFL jackets
- where do I buy NFL jackets online
- NFL jerseys
- NFL jerseys online
- NFL uniforms
- NFL uniforms online
- NFL jackets
- NFL jackets online

How to find keywords that will send traffic to your site.

Now you have a list of keywords, you need to understand how much traffic these keywords receive in Google. Without search traffic data, you could end up targeting keywords with zero searches. Armed with the right knowledge, you can target keywords with hundreds or even thousands of potential visitors every month.

First, you have to sign up for a free Google Adwords account, link provided below. Once signed in, you need to access the Keyword Planner tool.

To do this, sign in, click on 'Tools' in the top-menu, click on 'Keyword Planner', then click on 'Get search volume data and trends', copy and paste your keywords into the box. Select your country, and then click the blue 'Get search volume' button.

When you are finished, you will have the exact amount of times each keyword was searched for in Google.

Mmm. Fresh data. This is just the kind of data we need.

Now we know which keywords receive more searches than others, and more importantly, we know which keywords receive no searches at all. You can focus on keywords that will lead to traffic to your site.

| Ad group Ideas | Keyword Ideas | | | | | 📈 | ⬇ Download | Add all (4) |

Keyword (by relevance)		▼ Avg. monthly searches [?]	Competition [?]	Suggested bid [?]	Ad Impr. share [?]	Add to plan
football jerseys	📈	720	High	A$1.50	0%	»
football jerseys online	📈	320	High	A$1.13	0%	»
football jackets	📈	30	Medium	-	0%	»
where to buy football jerseys	📈	10	Medium	A$2.12	0%	»

Google Adwords
http://www.google.com/intl/en/adwords/

How to find keywords for easy rankings.

Now you need to find out how competitive your desired keywords are. Armed with an understanding of how competitive your desired keywords are, you can discover keywords your site can realistically achieve rankings for in Google.

Let's say you are a second-hand bookseller and you want to target 'book store online'. It's unlikely you are going to beat Amazon and Barnes and Noble.

But, maybe there's a gem hiding in your list very few people are targeting — maybe something like 'antique book stores online'.

You have the advantage if your competitors haven't thought of targeting your keyword. You simply have to do better SEO than they are doing and you have a really good chance at beating their rankings.

You need a way to wash this list and separate the ridiculously competitive keywords from the easy keywords no one has thought of.

There are many schools of thought on how to do this. The most popular competitive research practices are listed below, with my thoughts on each.

1. Manually going through the list, looking at the rankings, and checking if low-quality pages are appearing in the top results.

This is good for a quick glance to see how competitive a market is. However, it is unreliable and you need to supplement it with real data.

2. Look at how many search engine results are coming up in Google for your keyword.

The amount of results is listed just below the search box after you type in your keyword. This tactic is common in cheap online courses teaching SEO, but completely unreliable. This is my least favorite strategy.

The reason? There may be a very low amount of competing pages for a particular keyword, but the sites ranked at the top of the results could be unbeatable.

3. Using the competition score from the Google AdWords Keyword Research tool.

Don't be tempted. This is a common tool, lauded on the Internet as an easy way to judge SEO competitiveness for keywords, and it just simply doesn't work!

The competition score included in the Google AdWords Keyword Research tool is intended for AdWords only. It is an indication of how many advertisers are competing for the particular keyword through paid advertising. Completely irrelevant for SEO.

4. Using a competitive analysis tool, such as Moz's Keyword Difficulty tool.

To get a realistic idea of your chances of ranking high for a particular keyword, you need to understand the strength of the pages in the top-10.

A great tool for this is Moz's Keyword Difficulty tool.

With Moz's Keyword Difficulty tool, you can simply enter your keyword into their tool, click 'check difficulty', and then click 'view serp analysis reports' and it will show vital stats for pages appearing in the top-10.

Of these stats, the most important are # root domains linking to the page, and # root domains linking to the root domain. These two stats tell you how many unique sites are pointing to the specific page ranking, and how many unique sites are linking to anywhere in the site in general.

Next up, if you enter your own website into Moz's Open Site Explorer tool, you can see these same stats for your site, and then know how many links you need to beat the competition.

Armed with this knowledge, you can hunt around to find easy keywords with weak competition, and set targets for how many links you need for a top listing.

You can use Moz's Difficulty Tool by signing up for a 30-day free trial. There are not many alternative keyword tools out there providing a decent level of accuracy in my experience, however, another tool I have found useful is Market Samurai, which offers similar reports to Moz.

Moz - Keyword Difficulty Tool
https://moz.com/researchtools/keyword-difficulty

Moz – Open Site Explorer
https://moz.com/researchtools/ose/

Market Samurai
http://www.marketsamurai.com/

On-page SEO. How to let Google know what your page is about.

On-page SEO is the process of ensuring that your site is readable to search engines. Learning correct on-page SEO is not only important in ensuring Google picks up the keywords you want, but it is an opportunity to achieve easy wins and improve your site's overall performance.

On-page SEO includes the following considerations:

1. Making sure site content is visible to search engines.
2. Making sure your site is not blocking search engines
3. Making sure search engines pick up the keywords you want.

Most on-page SEO you can do yourself, if you have a basic level of experience dealing with sites.

If you are not technically inclined, please note there are technical sections of this chapter. You should still read these so you understand what has to be done to achieve rankings in Google, you can easily hire a web designer or web developer to implement the SEO techniques in this chapter, after you know what it takes to achieve top rankings.

How to structure your site for easy and automatic SEO.

These best practices will ensure your site is structured for better recognition by Google and other search engines.

1. Search engine friendly URLs.

Have you ever visited a web page and the URL looked like something like this...

http://www.examplesite.com/~articlepage21/post-entry321.asp?q=3

What a mess!

These kinds of URLs are a quick way to confuse search engines and site visitors. Clean URLs are more logical, user friendly, and search engine friendly.

Here is an example of a clean URL:

http://www.examplesite.com/football-jerseys

Much better.

Take a quick look at Google's search engine results. You will see a very large portion of sites in the top-10 have clean and readable URLs like the above example. And by a very large portion... I mean the vast majority.

Most site content management systems have search engine friendly URLs built into the site. It is often a matter of simply enabling the option in your site settings. If your site doesn't have search engine friendly URLs, it's time for a 'friendly' chat with your web developer to fix this up.

2. Internal navigation

There is no limit on how to structure the navigation of your site. This can be a blessing or a curse.

Some people force visitors to watch an animation or intro before they can even access the site. In the process, some sites make it harder for visitors and more confusing for search engines to pick up the content on the site.

Other sites keep it simple by having a menu running along the top of the site or running down the left-hand side of the browser window. This has pretty much become an industry standard for most sites.

By following this standard, you make it significantly easier for visitors and search engines to understand your site. If you intend to break this convention, you must understand it is likely you will make it harder for search engines to pick up all of the pages on your site.

As a general rule, making it easier for users makes it easier for Google.

Above all else, your web site navigation must be made of real text links — not images.

If your main site navigation is currently made up of images, slap your web designer and change them to text now! If you do not have the main navigation featured in text, your internal pages will almost be invisible to Google and other search engines.

For an additional SEO boost, include links to pages you want visible to search engines and visitors on the home page.

By placing links specifically on the home page, Google's search engine spider can come along to your site and quickly understand which pages on your site are important and worth including in the search results.

How to make Google pick up the keywords you want.

There are many misconceptions being circulated about what to do, and what not to do, when it comes to optimizing keywords into your page.

Some bloggers are going so far as telling their readers to not put keywords in the content of targeted pages at all. These bloggers — I'm not naming names — do have the best intentions and have really taken worry about Google's spam detection to the next level.

But it is complete madness.

Not having keywords on your page it makes it almost impossible for Google to match your page with the keyword you want to rank for. If Google completely devalued having keywords on the page, Google would be a crappy search engine.

Think about it. If you search for 'Ford Mustang 65 Auto Parts' and arrive on pages without those words on the page at all, it's extremely unlikely you have found what you're looking for.

Google needs to see the keywords on your page, and these keywords must be visible to your users. The easy approach is to either create content around your keyword, or naturally weave your keyword into the page. I'm not saying your page should look like the following example.

'Welcome to the NFL jersey store. Here we have NFL jersey galore, with a wide range of NFL jerseys including women's NFL jerseys, men's NFL jerseys and children's NFL jerseys and much much more.'

This approach may have worked 10 years ago, but not now. The keyword should appear naturally in your page. Any attempts to go bonkers with your keywords will look horrible and may set off spam filters in search engines. Use your keyword naturally throughout the content. Repeating your keyword a couple of times is more than enough.

It's really that simple.

Next up, you need to ensure you have a handful of LSI keywords on your page. LSI stands for Latent Semantic Indexing. Don't be discouraged by the technical term, 'LSI keywords' is an SEO term for related phrases. Google believes a page is more naturally written, and has a higher tendency to be good quality and relevant, if it also includes relevant and related keywords to your main phrase.

To successfully optimize a page, you need to have your main keywords and related keywords in the page. Find two or three related keywords to your main keyword, and repeat these in the page two or three times each. Ubersuggest is a great tool for finding keywords Google considers related to your main keywords — it does this by scraping suggestions from Google's auto-suggest box. Use Ubersuggest and your keyword research to determine a list of the most related keywords.

Ubersuggest – Free.
http://ubersuggest.org

Areas you can weave keywords into the page include:
-       Meta description and meta title tags.

- Navigation anchor text.
- Navigation anchor title tags.
- Headings (h1, h2, h3, and h4 tags).
- Content text.
- Bolded and italicized text.
- Internal links in content.
- Image filename, image alt tag and image title tag.
- Video filename, video title.

How to get more people clicking on your rankings in Google.

Meta tags have been widely misunderstood as mysterious pieces of code SEO professionals mess around with, and the secret to attaining top rankings. This couldn't be further from the truth.

The function of meta tags is really quite simple. Meta tags are bits of code on your site controlling how your site appears in Google.

If you don't fill out your meta tags, Google will automatically use text from your site to create your search listing. This is exactly what you don't want Google to do, otherwise it can end up looking like gibberish! Fill out these tags correctly, and you can increase the number of people clicking to your site from the search engine results.

Below is an example of the meta tag code.

<title>Paul's NFL Jerseys</title>

```
<meta description='Buy NFL jerseys online. Wide range of
colors and sizes.' />
<meta name="robots" content="noodp, noydir" />
```

Below is an example of how a page with the above meta
tag should appear as a search engine result in Google:

Paul's NFL Jerseys
Buy Paul's NFL jerseys online. Wide range of colors and
sizes.
http://www.yoursite.com/

Pretty simple, huh?

The title tag has a character limit of roughly 70 characters
in Google. Use anymore than 70 characters and it is likely
Google will truncate your title tag in the search engine
results.

The meta description tag has a character limit of roughly
155 characters. Just like the title tag, Google will shorten
your listing if it has any more than 155 characters in the
tag.

The last meta robots tag indicates to Google you want to
control how your listing appears in the search results. It's
good to include this, otherwise Google may ignore your
tags and instead use those listed on other directories such
as the Open Directory Project and the Yahoo Directory.

To change these tags on your site you have three options:

1. Use the software your site is built on. Most content management systems have the option to change these tags. If it doesn't, you may need to install a plugin to change these tags.

2. Speak with your web designer or web developer to manually change your Meta tags for you.

3. If you are a tech-savvy person and are familiar with HTML, you can change these tags in the code yourself.

Site load speed — Google magic dust.

How fast (or slow) your site loads is another factor Google takes into account when deciding how it should rank your pages in the search results.

A very well-known Google employee, Matt Cutts, publicly admitted fast load speed is a positive ranking factor.

If your site is as slow as a dead snail, then it is likely your site is not living up to its potential in the search engines. If your site load time is average, improving the load speed is an opportunity for an easy SEO boost.

Not only is load speed a contributing factor to achieving top rankings in Google, extensive industry reports have shown for each second shaved off a site, there is an average increase of 7% to the site conversion rate. In other words, the faster your site loads, the more chance you have of people completing a sale or filling out an inquiry form. Clearly this is not an aspect of your site to be overlooked.

Fortunately there are a handful of tools that make it easy to improve your load speed.

1. Google Page Speed Insights.
https://developers.google.com/speed/pagespeed/insights

Google's great free tool, Page Speed Insights, will give you a page load score out of 100. You can see how well your load speed compares to other sites. You can also see how well your site loads on mobile and desktop. Scores closer to 100 are near perfect.

After running a test on your site, the tool will give you a list of high priority, medium priority, and low priority areas for improvement. You can forward these on to your developer to speed up your site, or if you are a bit of a tech-head, you can have a crack at fixing these up yourself.

2. Pingdom Tools
http://tools.pingdom.com/

Pingdom Tools is great for an overview of how long your site takes to load in different areas of the world, and for a quick breakdown of files and resources that are slowing your site down.

After the test is completed, if you scroll down you will see a list of the files each visitor has to download each time they visit your site. If you discover files that can be decreased in size, you can improve your site load speed.

Easy targets for improvements are large images. If you have any images over 200kb, these can usually be optimized and shrunk down to a fraction of the size without any loss in quality. Take a note of these files, send them to your web developer or web designer, and ask them to compress the files to a smaller file size.

The usual suspects — sitemaps.xml and robots.txt

Sitemaps.xml

Search engines automatically look for a special file on each site called the sitemaps.xml file. Having this file on your site is a must for making it easy for search engines to discover pages on your site. Sitemaps are essentially a giant map to all of the pages on your site. Fortunately, creating this file and getting it on to your site is a straightforward process.

Most CMS sytems have a sitemaps file automatically generated. This includes systems like Wordpress, Magento, Shopify. If this is not the case on your site, you may need to install a plugin or use the free XML Sitemaps Generator tool. The XML Sitemaps Generator will automatically create a sitemaps.xml file for you.

XML Sitemaps Generator
http://www.xml-sitemaps.com

Next ask your web developer or web designer to upload it into the main directory of your site, or do it yourself if you have FTP access. Once uploaded, the file should be publicly accessible with an address like the below example:

http://www.yoursite.com/sitemaps.xml

Once you have done this, you should submit your sitemap to the Google Webmaster Tools account for your site.

If you do not have a Google Webmaster Tools account, the below article by Google gives simple instructions for web developers or web designers to set this up.

Add and verify a site to Google Webmaster Tools
http://support.google.com/webmasters/bin/answer.py?hl=en&answer=34592

Login to your account and click on your site. Under 'site configuration' click 'sitemaps', and in the textbox, enter the full address to your site.

Robots.txt

Another must-have for every site is a robots.txt file. This should sit in the same place as your sitemaps.xml file. The address to this file should look the same as the example below:

http://www.yoursite.com/robots.txt

The robots.txt file is a simple file that exists so you can tell the areas of your site you *don't* want Google to list in the search engine results.

There is no real boost from having a robots.txt file on your site. It is essential you check to ensure you don't have a robots.txt file blocking areas of your site you want search engines to find.

The robots.txt file is just a plain text document, its contents should look something like below:

robots.txt good example

User-agent: *
Disallow: /admin
User-agent: *
Disallow: /logs

If you want your site to tell search engines to not crawl your site, it should look like the next example. If you *do not* want your entire site blocked, you must make sure it does *not* look like the example below. It is always a good idea to double check it is not set up this way, just to be safe.

robots.txt - blocking the entire site

User-agent: *
Disallow: /

The forward slash in this example tells search engines their software should not visit the home directory.

To create your robots.txt file, simply create a plain text document with Notepad if you are on Windows, or Textedit if you are on Mac OS. Make sure the file is saved as a plain text document, and use the 'robots.txt good example' as an indication on how it should look. Take care to list any directories you do not want search engines to visit, such as internal folders for staff, admin areas, CMS back-end areas, and so on.

If there aren't any areas you would like to block, you can skip your robots.txt file altogether, but just double check you don't have one blocking important areas of the site like the above example.

Duplicate content — canonical tags and other fun.

In later chapters I will describe how Google Panda penalized sites with duplicate content. Unfortunately, many site content management systems will sometimes automatically create multiple versions of one page.

For example, let's say your site has a product page on socket wrenches, but because of the system your site is built on, the exact same page can be accessed from multiple URLs from different areas of your site:

http://www.yoursite.com/products.aspx?=23213
http://www.yoursite.com/socket-wrenches
http://www.yoursite.com/tool-kits/socket-wrenches

In the search engine's eyes this is confusing as hell and multiple versions of the page are considered duplicate content.

To account for this, you should always ensure a special tag is placed on every page in your site, called the 'rel canonical' tag.

The rel canonical tag indicates the original version of a web page to search engines. By telling Google the page you consider to be the 'true' version of the page into the tag, you can indicate which page you want listed in the search results.
Choose the URL providing the most sense to users and the best SEO benefit, this should usually be the URL that reads like plain English.

Using the earlier socket wrenches example, with the tag below, Google would be more likely to display the best version of the page in the search engine results.

```
<link rel="canonical
" href="http://www.yoursite.com/socket-wrenches
"/>
```

As a general rule, include this tag on every page on your site, shortly before the </head> tag in the code.

Usability — the new SEO explained.

As mentioned in the first chapter, the trust and relevancy of sites has become increasingly important for Google. Market share for mobile and tablet Internet users skyrocketed to over 29% in 2015 — to keep search a good experience for all users, Google has started to give preference to sites providing a good user experience for users on all devices. Usability has taken an increased importance in the SEO industry as a result, as SEO pundits found you can get an advantage by making your site easy to use.

For example, let's say a mobile user is searching for late night pizza delivery in Los Angeles. One local business has a site with a large amount of backlinks but no special support for mobile users, it's difficult for the user to navigate around the site because it doesn't automatically 'fit' to the screen, and the navigation text is small and hard to use on a touch screen.

Another competing local business has low amounts of backlinks, but good support for mobile users. Its design fits perfectly to the screen and has special navigation for mobile users, making it easy to get around.

In many cases, the second site will rank higher than the first, for mobile users. This is just one example of how usability can have a significant impact on your rankings.

While a term like 'usability' can understandably seem a little vague, let's look at practical steps to improve your usability and the SEO strength of your site.

1. Make your site accessible for all devices.

Make your site accessible and easy for all users: desktop, mobile and tablet. The simple way to do this is to make sure your site is responsive, which means it automatically resizes across all devices and has mobile-friendly navigation for mobile users. Mobile support is covered in more detail in Bonus Chapter 2 in the Mobile SEO Update section, but you can enter your site into the below tool to quickly see if Google registers your site as 'mobile friendly'.

Mobile friendly Test.
https://www.google.com/webmasters/tools/mobile-friendly/

2. Increase your content quality.

Gone are the days of hiring a bunch of writers in India to bulk out the content on your site. It needs to be proofread and edited, and the more 'sticky' you make your content, the better result you will get. If you provide compelling content, users will spend more time on your site and are less likely to 'bounce' back to the search results. Users will also be much more likely to share your content. Google will see this and give your rankings a boost.

3. Use clean code in your site.

There's a surprisingly high amount of sites with dodgy code, difficult for both search engines and Internet browsers to read. If there are HTML code errors in your site, which means, if it hasn't been coded according to industry best practices, it's possible your design will break when your site is viewed on different browsers, or even worse, confuse search engines when they come along and look at your site. Run your site through the below tool and ask your web developer to fix any errors.

Web standards validator
https://validator.w3.org/

4. Take it easy on the popups and advertisements.

Sites with spammy and aggressive ads are often ranked poorly in the search results. The SEO gurus have reached no consensus on the amount of ads leading to a penalty from Google, so use your common sense. Ensure advertisements don't overshadow your content and occupy the majority of screen real estate.

5. Improve the overall 'operability' of your site.

Does your site have slow web hosting, or a bunch of broken links and images? Simple technical oversights like these contribute to a poor user experience.

Make sure your site is with a reliable web hosting company and doesn't go down in peak traffic. Even better, make sure your site is hosted on a server in your local city, and this will make it faster for local users.

Next up, chase up any 404-errors with your web developer. 404 errors are errors indicating users are clicking on links in your site and being sent to an empty page. It contributes to a poor user experience, in Google's eyes, when we have broken links on a site sending users to error pages. Fortunately, these errors are easy fixed.

You can find 404 errors on your site by logging into your Google Webmaster Tools account, clicking on your site, then clicking on 'Crawl' and 'Crawl Errors'. Here you will find a list of 404 errors. If you click on the error and then click 'Linked From' you can find the pages with the broken links. Fix these yourself, or discuss with your web developer. You can usually clear a website of 404 errors quite quickly.

Google Webmaster Tools
https://www.google.com/webmasters/tools/

If you want external tools to speed up improving your site's usability, I have found these two resources helpful:

BrowserStack. Free to try, plans start at $29 per month.
https://www.browserstack.com

BrowserStack allows you to test your site on over +700 different browsers at once. You can preview how your site works on tablets, mobile devices, and all the different browsers such as Chrome, Firefox, Safari, Internet Explorer, and so on. It's helpful for making sure it displays correctly across many different devices.

Try My UI. Free to try, additional test results start at $35. http://www.trymyui.com

Try My UI provides videos, audio narration, surveys of users going through your site, and reports on any difficulties they uncover. Usability tests are good for larger projects requiring objective feedback from normal users. The first test result is free, making Try My UI a good usability test provider to start with.

Readability — SEO for the future.

One of the strongest ranking factors has been flying under the radar, overlooked by many SEO professionals in their optimization checklists, leaving a golden opportunity for those that know about it. I'm talking about readability.

Google have been outspoken about readability as an important consideration for webmasters. Google's SEO spam king himself, Matt Cutts, has gone on to say that poorly researched and misspelled content will rank poorly, and clarity should be your focus. And by readability, this means not just avoiding spelling mistakes, but making your content readable for the widest possible audience, with simple language and sentence structures.

Flesch readability has since surfaced in the Searchmetrics'
Google ranking factors report, showing a high correlation
between high ranking sites and easy to read content. The
Searchmetrics rankings report discovered that sites
appearing in the top-10 showing an average Flesch
reading score of 76.00 — content that is fairly easy to read
for 13-15 year old students and up.

It makes sense readability is a concern for Google. By
encouraging search results to have content readable to a
wide audience, Google maximise their advertising
revenues. If Google were to encourage complicated results
that mostly appeal to a smaller demographic, such as post-
graduates, it would lower Google's general appeal and
their market share.

You can achieve an on-page SEO boost, while also
increasing your user engagement, by making your content
readable to a wide audience. Run your content through a
Flesch readability test. It will look at your word and
sentence usage, and give you a score on how readable it is.
Scores between 90-100 are easily understood by an 11-year
old student, 60-70 easily understood by 13- to 15-year old
students, and 0-30 best understood by University
graduates. You can use the free tool below, and should
aim for a readability score between 60-100. To improve
your score, edit your content to use fewer words per
sentence, and use words with a smaller number of
syllables.

Readability Score
https://readability-score.com

How to accelerate traffic and rankings with fresh content.

The most overlooked, but powerful, on-page SEO strategy is adding more unique, fresh content to your site. If you consistently add new pages to your site, you are going to receive more traffic. In fact, not only can you increase your traffic, you can receive an *exponential* traffic increase as you publish more content.

It's a no-brainer when you think about it. This is why blogs, publishing and news-type sites consistently get good results in search engines. More content means more rankings, more visitors, and more sales. Let's look at getting started with improving your traffic by adding fresh content.

1. Post new content on a regular schedule.

If you are going to add new content to your site, you need to decide on a schedule and stick to it. This might seem obvious, but you would be surprised at the large number of businesses that talk about starting a blog and never get around to it. It's the businesses with a regular roster of adding content to their site that see regular increases in search rankings, increases in overall search engine performance, and a growing loyal audience. Without a dedicated roster or schedule, it will never get done. Create a schedule for adding new content, and stick to it.

If you don't have the capacity to create content yourself, or a budget to hire a full-time marketing assistant to create content, try hiring a ghostwriter.

Good quality writers can be sourced between $25-$75 USD per article and you can regularly churn out fresh content to your heart's content. Popular services can put you in touch with talented writers, such as Textbroker or the Problogger job board.

Textbroker
https://www.textbroker.com

Problogger Job Board
http://jobs.problogger.net

2. Leverage your social media accounts.

It almost goes without saying, but you should be leveraging social media to drive traffic to new posts or pages added to your site.

Whenever you post new content, post it across all of your social media accounts. Then post it again in a couple of days and you will expose your content to a different segment of fans. You'll increase your social activity and as a result get higher rankings.

3. Link up your site to blog aggregators.

Blog directories are an easy opportunity for high-quality backlinks, available for anyone running blog. A handful of large authority blog directories accept site submissions and syndicate content — an opportunity to build up referral traffic. Simply ensure you have a base level of content to start, and then submit your site. A link to your to your blog can be approved within a week or two.

Here's a handful of high-quality blog directories accepting submissions:

http://www.technorati.com
http://www.alltop.com
http://www.blogarama.com
http://blogs.botw.org

~

That sums it up for the on-page SEO chapter.

If you have a small business, the technical factors mentioned earlier in this chapter are what will make the difference — such as ensuring your site has the right keywords and is accessible for all users.

If you are doing SEO for a large company and need a large amount of traffic, regularly publishing new content and ensuring structural areas of your site are setup correctly are what will make the difference — such as regularly posting new blog posts, ensuring you have sitemaps working correctly, and no duplicate content or 404 errors.

What's most important is you act. On-page SEO is often the easiest part of SEO. The power is in your hands to fix up these areas in your site, remember that small tweaks can lead to big results. Put these methods to practice and start improving your rankings.

Link building. How to rank extremely high on Google.

Why is link building so important?

The previous chapter described how to make your site visible to search engines and how to optimize keywords by using on page SEO. If you want to see your rankings improve by leaps and bounds, then your site needs links.

You may have wondered what makes link building so important, especially when there are so many factors Google use to rank sites.

The truth is, links are such a strong factor, it is unlikely you will rank high for a keyword if you are competing against sites with more backlinks.

When you think about it, links are the currency of the web. Each time a page links to another, it is a vote for the value of the page being linked to. If a page provides massive value to Internet users, it stands to reason it will be linked to from other sites. This is why links are such a strong factor in Google's algorithm.

Link building is the key to ranking your site high in the search engine results.

The dirty little secret no-one wants to tell you about link building.

There are a lot of opinions circulating the Internet about the best kind of links to build to your site. So much so, they often escalate into heated discussions.

What is the best link? A link from a government site or from a high trafficked blog? Is it better to get a link from a highly relevant site or from a site with a lot of social media activity?

The dirty secret no-one wants to tell you about link building is *there is no single best kind of link.*

If this weren't the case, Google wouldn't work. Everyone would go out and find a way to spam their way to the top of the rankings very quickly. Having thousands of one type of link pointing to a page is suspicious and a clear sign the site owner is gaming the system.

That said, as a rule, you should try to build links on authoritative, relevant and high-quality sites. High-quality, relevant links are much stronger than links from low-quality, unrelated sites.

How to acquire links and what to avoid in link building.

There are many stories floating around about business owners being slammed by Google for no good reason. Don't let the horror stories mislead you.

In most cases, what really happened is the webmaster was doing something clearly suspicious or out-dated, like building thousands of links to their site from link directories, and then their rankings suddenly dropped off from Google's top-10 search results.

If you don't exhibit overly spammy behavior in your link building, as a general rule you will be OK.

These best practices will ensure you acquire links correctly and don't break Google's terms of service:

1. Acquire links naturally and evenly over time. Your links should be attained consistently and organically. Don't go out and buy one thousand links pointing to your site in one week.

3. As a rule, don't purchase links. Buying links with the intention of boosting your rankings is against Google's terms of service and you risk being penalized. These kinds of links may work, but are generally not worth the potential damage, unless you are confident you know what you are doing.

5. Forget about link-swapping or link-trading schemes. These are completely obvious to Google, and either no longer work or may even may harm your site. This goes against common knowledge, but I've achieved countless number one rankings for ridiculously competitive keywords without ever swapping links. Link-swapping is extremely time-consuming and completely unnecessary. Get by without it.

6. Don't spam message boards or article sites with crappy content. This might work temporarily, but strategies like these are typically outdated very quickly.

7. There are paid networks out there offering to build new links to your site for a low monthly fee each month. Never use them. These networks are against Google's terms of service and using them is a quick way to ensure you find yourself in hot water with Google.

Anchor text. What's all the fuss?

There has been some controversy around anchor text, as touched on in a previous chapter. Anchor text *was* one of the strongest factors for achieving top rankings.

If you are wondering what anchor text is, anchor text is the text contained in a link.

If you had one thousand links to your site with 'NFL football jerseys' as the link text, and competitors only had a handful of links with the same anchor text, it was likely you would rank number one. That is, until Google's Penguin update effectively put an end for SEOs using 'exact match' anchor text as their strategy. Now it is just simply too risky.

Not only is it no longer as effective as it once was, building hundreds of 'exact match' links to a site actually can prevent it from ranking for that keyword.

So then, you might wonder, what is the best way to build up anchor text?

It should be natural.

It is OK to have your targeted keyword in your anchor text, but it should not be the only keyword or the main keyword in all of your links, and there should be a mix of related keywords.

If you think about it, this is a pattern all legitimate sites naturally attract. It defies logic that a quality site would automatically be linked with the exact same text throughout the entire World Wide Web.

Look over the below examples to see a bad anchor text profile compared to a natural anchor text profile:

Bad anchor text – external links
http://www.examplefootballbrand.com/football-jerseys.html
NFL football jerseys - 200 links

Good anchor text
http://www.examplefootballbrand.com/football-jerseys.html
examplefootballbrand – 50 links
NFL football jersey store - 10 links
NFL football jerseys- 5 links
http://www.example.com - 25 links
football jersey store - 5 links
football jerseys online - 5 links
football jacket store - 15 links
click here - 7 links
website – 15 links

The above good anchor text example illustrates the natural way sites accumulate links over time. Your target keyword should not be the most linked phrase to the page.

You can learn a lot by looking at the search engine results ranking in Google, enter high-ranking sites into Open Site Explorer, and looking at their anchor text. You'll notice almost every top-ranking page has natural anchor text, like the good example above.

Track your link-building efforts and keep them in a spreadsheet. This way you can monitor your anchor text and make sure it fits in with best practices.

Open Site Explorer
https://moz.com/researchtools/ose/

Simple link building strategies.

The link building strategies below will help you build up quality links pointing to your site, and give Google a nudge to rank your site higher.

Directory links.

Directory links are a tried and true form of link building that received some flack in recent years. This is due to Google penalizing spammers who built ridiculous amounts of low-quality directory links to their site.

Directory links shouldn't be overlooked. In fact, directory links should be the first place to start with any link building project. There's a solid amount of high-quality business directories where you can get powerful and strong backlinks built with a minimum of effort.

But just to be safe, your directory links should not make up much more than 10-20% of your total links. They must also be relevant and quality sites, i.e. not sites with web addresses like seolinksdirectory.com or freelinksdirectory.com. Sites like these just smell of spam! Before building a link on a directory, ask yourself: 'Does this look like a legitimate and trustworthy website?' If the answer is no, then move on and focus on legitimate, quality sites only.

If you work within these guidelines, you will not run afoul of any Google penalties.

To find relevant directories, use the below search terms in Google, replacing 'keyword' with your targeted keyword or industry, and you can find relevant directories for your niche:

keyword + submit
keyword + add url
keyword + add link
keyword + directory
keyword + resources

Here is a short list of business directories to get you started:

http://www.manta.com/claim
http://www.linkedin.com/company/add/show
http://www.hotfrog.com/AddYourBusiness.aspx
http://www.angieslistbusinesscenter.com
http://www.merchantcircle.com/signup
http://www.citysearch.com
https://biz.yelp.com

Stealing competitors' links.

Stealing competitors' links is an old-school tactic receiving a resurgence in recent times, due to Google's increased focus on links from quality sites, making it more difficult to find easy link opportunities.

If your competitor has done all the heavy lifting, why not take advantage of their hard work. Use the below sites to export your competitors' backlinks. By looking through their links you can often find link opportunities to build links pointing to your site. In most cases, you can be confident you are going after SEO-friendly link sources if the competitor is already ranking well in Google.

Ahrefs Backlink Checker – Free to try, then $79 per month.
http://www.ahrefs.com

Majestic SEO Backlink Checker – Free to try, then $49 per month.
https://majestic.com

Open Site Exporer – Free to try, then $99 per month
https://moz.com/researchtools/ose/

Video link building.

Google loves videos, and it especially loves videos from video powerhouse YouTube. If you want the opportunity to capture visitors from the world's largest video search engine, posting videos will considerably help your SEO.

Post relevant how-to guides, industry news updates, and instructional videos for the best response from users. Then link to relevant pages on your site in the description.

The key to success in video link building is to ensure the video and your description are related. You should aim to have your targeted keyword or relevant keywords occurring on the page somewhere.

And don't worry. Your video doesn't have to be on par with the latest Martin Scorsese masterpiece. It can be a simple 5 or 10-minute video, educating visitors with useful knowledge about your topic. Just focus on making it contribute value for the viewer.

The tools below can help with quickly creating videos and uploading them to the web.

Screenr
http://www.screenr.com
Screenr is a free video recording web app allowing you to record high-quality screencasts from the convenience of your own web browser. You can download the video files in high quality after you have finished, and it works on both Windows and Mac computers.

High-quality sites you can easily visit, upload videos and get backlinks from:

http://www.youtube.com
http://www.veoh.com
http://www.dailymotion.com
http://www.metacafe.com
http://www.youku.com
http://www.archive.org

Link bait.

Link bait is a new and effective strategy for building high-quality and powerful links on a large scale. Link bait is great because you create content once, but you can have thousands of people over the Internet sharing and linking to your content, while you sit back and put your feet up.

But what is link bait exactly? Link bait is any kind of compelling content that naturally acquires links from other sites as a result.

While there is an art to creating link bait successfully, you would be surprised at how easy it is to earn links and social media activity with this strategy.

You need to make your content free and shareable. Your content must be so valuable it would almost be worth paying for.

To create this content, you should use your expertise or even hire researchers to put together juicy industry content that lends itself to being shared.

Wrap up this content into a whitepaper, top-10 list, an easy to understand infographic, or a downloadable resource and you have made it compelling for visitors to read and to share.

Once you have created your content, you have to promote your content to kick off.

Promote this content heavily through your site and social media accounts. Prompt readers to share the post at the bottom of the content. Make sharing the content as easy as possible and you will maximize results.

Next up, find popular link bait in your industry or niche. Then use a link analysis tool such as Ahrefs or Open Site Explorer to pull a list of sites linking to popular content in your niche. Send out a quick email blast to site owners and bloggers to let them know about your bigger and better resource.

If you really want to take link baiting to the next level, write and publish a compelling press release about your link bait content. With a press release, it can be exposed to thousands of journalists and potentially has a chance of attracting media coverage.

You might be wondering what a successful link baiting campaign looks like. I've listed examples below:

WordPress SEO Guide
https://yoast.com/articles/wordpress-seo/
Joost de Valk is well known in the SEO industry, largely due to his one page guide to WordPress SEO that is updated every month or so. This guide has earned many links and shares over many years.

101 Motivational Business Quotes
http://www.quicksprout.com/2009/12/07/101-motivational-business-quotes/
Excellent example of a great link bait article that went viral, and could be outsourced for pennies on the dollar.

Types of link bait:
- Infographics
- How-to guides
- Beginner guides
- Breaking news
- Top 10 lists
- Industry reports

Pictochart. Free to start.
http://ww.piktochart.com
Great service for infographic generation, has an easy drag
and drop interface to put infographics together in minutes.

Prlog.
http://www.prlog.org
Prlog offers entry-level free press release syndication
services, with additional coverage for an added fee.

PRNewswire.
http://www.prnewswire.com
Many PR firms will simply write a press release and then
release it to PRNewswire and charge a premium for doing
so. Cut out the middleman, write up your press release
yourself, and you can get massive PR for a fraction of the
cost of hiring a PR agent. Packages start at $425 USD and
scale up for increased syndication.

Broken link building/link outreach.

Broken link building is a new, but effective strategy. With this new strategy, you can reach out to quality sites with broken links on their pages, and use this as an opportunity to convince the site administrator to provide an updated link to your site.

When you find a broken link, let them know the broken link exists and you have an alternative resource on your site that will benefit their readers. With this strategy you should create a linkable resource on your site. This makes it very easy for the webmaster to point the link to your replacement.

Use the formulas below to find potential pages with broken links, replacing 'keyword' with the keyword you are targeting:

keyword useful links
keyword useful resources
keyword useful sites
keyword recommended links
keyword recommended resources
keyword recommended sites
keyword suggested links
keyword suggested resources
keyword suggested sites
keyword more links
keyword more resources
keyword more sites
keyword related links
keyword related resources

keyword related sites

If you want to automate this process, the service below
will do the heavy lifting, and give you a list of sites with
broken links and contact details so you can quickly reach
out to the webmaster.

Broken linkbuilding. $67 monthly.
http://www.brokenlinkbuilding.com
This tool is comprehensive, but comes at a price. By typing
in keywords you are targeting, the broken link building
tool will find a solid amount of broken link opportunities.
Saves time and finds quality opportunities.

Broken brand mentions.

Broken brand mentions is a fast, simple and reliable form
of link building you can use for almost every SEO project.
It goes like this: in some cases, when someone mentions
your brand they forget to post a link. Track mentions of
your brand, and where suitable, reach out and ask for a
link back to your site. Use the below tools to track
mentions of your brand. If you see a mention of your
brand without a link, send a quick email to the author, and
they will often be happy to link to your site.

Brand monitoring sites I've found useful:

Social Mention. Free to try.
http://www.socialmention.com

Social Mention is a very powerful brand monitoring tool. At the writing of this book, you cannot receive email alerts. Social Mention is completely free and powerful, so it's worth checking out.

Mention. Free to try, pricing starts at £29 per month. https://en.mention.com
Mention is a powerful brand-monitoring tool that will send an email alert when your brand is mentioned online, so you can respond quickly.

Paid links

While Google 'paid' links are against their terms-of-service, these below link building tactics do work and can fly under the radar. Needless to say, if you're feeling daring, you've been warned and I take no responsibility for what happens as a result of paid link strategies.

Donate to charities & non-profits.

Charities and non-profits sites often have a donors page. Search for "site:.org + donors" or "site:.org + sponsors" in Google for a list of organizations that have these pages, offer a donation, and request a listing on the page.

Better Business Bureau.

Links from the Better Business Bureau are among the best links you can receive. Better Business Bureau links will pass authority and trust. Check your listing to see if you are already linking back to your site, and if you're not already a member, then consider signing up.

Advanced link building.

The aforementioned link building techniques are enough for about 90% of readers to push rankings higher than competitors. For link building junkies who've exhausted the above options, here's a handful of strategies listed quickly in rapid-fire fashion. These are intended for advanced SEO users, who are actively blogging or have an established social media presence.

1. Create a Twitter profile.

Adding a link in a Twitter profile is a big opportunity disguised as a small opportunity. Simply by creating a Twitter profile, and listing your website in both the 'website' and 'bio' fields, you will get a handful of links from high domain authority aggregators that scrape your information from Twitter. Sites that do this include Klout, Twellow, Twitter Counter, and many others. To make these links more powerful, you can make your profile active without a large overhead of time. Use a service such as Hootsuite to auto-post blog posts from RSS feeds relevant to your niche, to make your profile active. Build up a base level of followers to your account with a small budget with a service like Twitter Ads or Twitter Counter - Featured Users.

Hootsuite
http://www.hootsuite.com

Twitter Ads
https://ads.twitter.com

Twitter Counter – Featured Users
http://twittercounter.com/pages/featured

2. Pingback & trackback link building targeting authority sites.

You can get a handful of easy-win authority links, including .edu and .gov links, by linking out to blogs in your industry with pingbacks enabled. Pingbacks are notifications from your blog sent to other blogs when you mention an external post. Blogs with pingbacks enabled will show a link back to your website in their comment section when this happens.

Here's how a comment will look if it is a trackback or pingback:

Digital nomad blog
[...]read the latest tips on how to travel with only your carry on luggage[...]

Pingbacks build up valuable relevant links back to your website. They can also be a traffic source, picking up engaged readers from other sites and sending them to your site.

Run a quick search on Google to find the top-50 or top-100 blogs in your industry, then go through and find the ones with trackbacks enabled. For example, to find digital nomad blogs, you might type into Google:

intitle:"digital nomad" "comment"

Next up, in your upcoming blog posts, link out to blogs with pingbacks enabled. For this to work successfully, keep in mind you need to link out to actual posts, not the home page.

3. Create your own authority links.

The most powerful link building strategy is to simply go out and make your own authority links. By buying a previously owned website or domain, you can turn it into a blog and unlimited source for powerful, highly relevant links back to your site.

There are readers out there who will scoff at this strategy and there are readers out there nodding their heads — it's the readers nodding their heads that know how powerful this strategy is. Links from authority sources in your market are much more powerful than any other kind of link, and the easiest way to get authority links is to create your own authority site. Consider buying a website more than three or four years old with a relevant domain, for a more powerful effect.

Flippa.
https://flippa.com
Market place for buying and selling websites.

Sedo
https://sedo.com
Buy and sell domains.

4. Relationship link building.

If you've been following the online advice on blogging and link building in the past couple of years you will have noticed a recurring theme: building relationships with other bloggers in your industry is a powerful way to earn strong backlinks to your site.

While this strategy is only relevant for users with active blogs on their site, fortunately, creating these relationships and getting the links is easier than it sounds. Other bloggers in your industry are just as dependent on links as you are. By linking out in your blog posts to other bloggers you 1) give a valuable backlink to the blogger, and 2) give recognition to the blogger for being an authority in the industry. Everyone likes recognition, and the law of reciprocity comes into play here, you will find most bloggers are grateful for being mentioned and happy to link back in a social media post or future blog post.

Try creating or curating popular blog posts into a top-level summary, then send a quick email to the bloggers mentioned, let them know, and very politely ask for a mention or linkback. The best part of this strategy is curating blog posts; it is often easier than creating content from scratch.

Example email:
'Hey [expert blogger]
Just thought I'd give you a heads up. I've just featured you in my post [xyz]…

Hope you don't mind. If you're happy with the article, would really love a mention on social media or perhaps a link back. Or if you want anything changed, feel free to let me know.
Really enjoyed your post on [xyz].
Cheers'

Example expert round-up post:
Experienced business travellers reveal their favorite travel tips
http://www.businessinsider.sg/business-travel-tips-from-expert-travelers-2015-6/

5. Testimonial link building.

An awesome way to get high quality, relevant links back to your site is to give out testimonials. Sometimes you can actually earn a link back to your site from somebody else's homepage, possibly one of the strongest types of links to get! I will sometimes so far as purchasing a product just to get a testimonial link. Give this strategy a try by finding a few sites with testimonials and offering your own. Of course make it easy for the webmaster by including all the information they need, such as a photo, your name, job title, testimonial and link back to your site. The key is to look for businesses or services already with a testimonials page, or a testimonials carousel or widget on their homepage. Speed up your search with a couple of Google search queries:

"keyword" +testimonials
"keyword" +recommendations
"keyword" +"client testimonials"
"keyword" +"what customers say"

Social media & SEO.

Is social media important for SEO?

Social media has become integral to the way we use the Internet. Important content is not only linked, it is shared, liked, tweeted, and pinned. How people use the Internet has drastically changed, and this hasn't gone unnoticed at the Googleplex. Many of the independent studies on Google's ranking algorithm show a large correlation with high-ranking pages having strong social media activity.

While the official stance from Google is that they do not 'directly' use social signals in their algorithm, the SEO community pretty much agrees it is a strong factor in achieving rankings. Disagreements aside, I can tell from personal experience, sites with large social followings get much higher rankings in a shorter timeframe by a mile.

Not only can you use social media to build social activity to increase your overall SEO strength, you can use social media to regularly create backlinks that are free and easy to build. It also increases referral traffic back to your site and engages previous customers. As a rule, social media should be a part of every SEO project.

Google+ & SEO.

Google has been consistently rewarding businesses using their own social network with higher rankings. To be specific, Google+ is reported as one of strongest ranking factors for the past several years, so much so, if you look at the SEO ranking factor surveys, Google+ is consistently at the top of the list!

A lot of businesses still aren't using Google+, so this is an opportunity to get an advantage over competitors. At a minimum, you should set up a business page and add some posts to your profile. Next up, encourage followers by adding a Google+ follow button on your website, and link to your Google+ page in your email footer. Social media management is beyond the scope of this book, but simply getting started and building a base level of activity on Google+ will put yourself ahead of other businesses — it is the social media site most often overlooked by many brands, and you can use this to your advantage. Get started with the below links:

Google – My Business
https://www.google.com/business/

Google+ Follow Button
https://developers.google.com/+/web/follow/

Facebook & SEO.

Facebook is the world's most popular social network. What's popular on Facebook is essentially a snapshot of public opinion, and Google have noted this by making Facebook activity a very strong factor in their algorithm. You should consider using Facebook for every SEO project. If you only have the time or budget to use one social network in your SEO strategy, use Facebook.

To improve your site's Facebook social activity, share content from your own site on your Facebook page on a regular basis.

Each time you do this, you receive more exposure from your fan base, and you also build up social activity around the content on your site. Be careful to mix this up with relevant, engaging non-commercial content for your user base, so you don't turn them off and maintain high levels of engagement. Examples include infographics, inspirational quotes, inspirational photos, and so on.

Build up your audience by including a Facebook follow button on your site, your email signatures, and your thank you or success pages.

If you want to speed up building your audience, you can use Facebook advertising to build a relevant audience of local customers. This is a good strategy if your competitors in the rankings have a larger following and you are looking to beat them. You can also use Facebook advertising to increase exposure for your posts, or even run advertising campaigns to for a promotional offer. Facebook advertising stands out as a great way to build up an audience, social activity and referral sales for projects with a budget.

Facebook for business
https://www.facebook.com/business

Facebook advertising
https://en-gb.facebook.com/business/products/ads

Twitter & SEO.

Twitter is filled with discussion on the world's latest news and events. In many cases, groundbreaking news stories are released on Twitter before the world's major news outlets. The death of Osama Bin Laden is the perfect example — it was leaked on Twitter by a former chief of staff to the US Defense Secretary and within minutes it was all over the news.

Google have recognized this and use Twitter activity in their algorithm. While it may not be as strong as other social networks, you can use Twitter to build up your overall SEO strength. Twitter is a great social network to weave into your SEO strategy as you can schedule a lot of your tweets in advance without coming across as too spammy, and manage your account with only a small commitment of time and effort.

Schedule tweets to your pages such as Hootsuite and start building up your tweet counts on your pages. Mix this up with relevant and informative tweets about your industry. You should aim for a maximum of 12 tweets per day. 12 Tweets per day is roughly the limit you can post without annoying your followers. If you're lazy like me, you can schedule all of your tweets about 3-months in advance.

If you want to encourage site visitors to tweet your content for you, include a 'tweet this page' link on every page or blog post on your web site.

Tweetdeck. Free.
http://www.tweetdeck.com

Free and easy Twitter management software. You can install Tweetdeck on your computer and manage your whole Twitter account from inside the program. Popular features include managing multiple accounts, scheduling tweets, and arranging feeds so you only see updates from Twitterers you're interested in.

Hootsuite. Free to start. $10 monthly for power users.
http://www.hootsuite.com

More advanced than Tweetdeck, you can use Hootsuite to schedule tweets, analyze social media traffic, manage multiple accounts, create social media reports to monitor your success, and much more. Recommended for power users or automating multiple accounts.

Other social networks.

Let's face it, we'd all love to play around on social networks all day, but we don't have the spare time to be always looking for great ideas and sharing them endlessly on social media accounts.

If you have limited resources, focus on Facebook, Google+ and Twitter.

If you are looking for an extra edge, doing SEO for a large brand, or maybe you have an army of helpers waiting for your command, you can gain significant boosts by expanding your social activity to several social media sites.

Setup an account on the below networks, posting on the networks most relevant to your business:

LinkedIn
http://www.linkedin.com

LinkedIn is the Facebook for professionals. LinkedIn is a fantastic networking tool if you are in the business-to-business industry and looking to build up your personal brand or the brand of your site. If you want to increase your effectiveness on Linkedin, join groups and participate in discussions, post relevant updates about your industry and post content in the news feed.

Pinterest
http://www.pinterest.com

Pinterest has become one of the fastest-growing social networks in a very short timeframe. Pinterest's fast-growing user base is primarily made up of women. The site has effectively turned into a giant shopping list of wish-list items. If your target audience is women, you should be on Pinterest.

Instagram
http://www.instagram.com

Initially a mobile app to help users make their photos look pretty, Instagram has skyrocketed from a fledgling mobile app to competing with major social networks in just a few years. Instagram limits the amount of links you can post, which essentially means the links from your profile on Instagram are much more powerful. If you work in a fashion or image-heavy industry, Instagram is a must-have social network to incorporate into your SEO and overall digital strategy.

Social media analytics.

If you invest time and effort building up your social media profiles, you will want to track your results so you can separate the parts of your strategy that are successful and not so successful.

Social media analytics is different compared to other web analytics, because social analytics are geared to measuring the conversation and interaction of your fan base with your brand. Using the software listed below, you can monitor results and get valuable insights on how to improve your social media efforts:

Sprout Social. Free for 30-days. $59 per month for regular use.
http://sproutsocial.com/features

A great web analytics and social media management package that allows you to track the performance of your social media profiles over time. Sprout Social has a free trial, suited to advanced level use and offers powerful analytic reports for major social networks.

Hootsuite. Free plan available. Paid plans start at $10 per month.
https://hootsuite.com/products/social-media-analytics
Hootsuite is quoted many times in this book and for good reason — Hootsuite is a robust social media management software allowing for control over many social networks, as well as powerful web analytics insights. Its paid plans are also quite affordable for pro-users.

Google Analytics Social Tracking. Free
http://www.google.com/analytics/

Google Analytics social-tracking features are great for
tracking basic social interactions that occur when visitors
are on your site. It is free and includes out-of-the-box with
the standard setup. To see social reports, log in to Google
Analytics, click on the Acquisition tab in the main menu,
then Social.

Web analytics in a nutshell. How to measure your success.

Web analytics changed how we do business in the 21st century. Now we can find valuable insights into customers, including demographics and behavior, insights that were previously difficult or impossible to discover. Now we can get extremely accurate insights into marketing performance at a granular level. We can find out what works and what doesn't, cut under performing marketing campaigns and increase budgets for winning campaigns. Simply put, web analytics have made it easier to grow almost any business. Read on for a quick guide covering the nuts and bolts of web analytics, and how to put web analytics to work for your business.

Why use Google Analytics?

You may have already heard about Google Analytics. Google Analytics is the web analytics platform used by the majority of sites. It has its quirks, but it's the best readily available, all-round analytics tool available for understanding site traffic. And the best part is it's free.

If you don't have Google Analytics installed, put down this book, install Google Analytics now and then slap your web developer. I'm not joking. Without Google Analytics set up, growing a business online is like trying to pilot an airplane blindfolded. Without Google Analytics it's difficult to find out what works and what doesn't, identify issues and solve them before they turn into bigger issues, and get a sense for the general direction your business is headed. This is applicable to about 90% of businesses.

To get started with Google Analytics, head on over to the below URL and click on 'sign in'. Create a Google account if you do not have one already, and walk through the simple steps to get started. You may need help from your web developer if you are unable to edit the code on your website.

Google Analytics
http://www.google.com/analytics/

How to use Google Analytics.

Let me tell you something a little risqué. On its own, most data is useless. You heard correctly, for real awareness and insights, we need to be able to compare data and identify trends over time. There are two ways to analyze and understand data in Google Analytics in reference to time:

1. Compare two date ranges.

Click on the date field input in Google Analytics. Enter two timeframes and you can compare them both. Useful date comparisons include comparing this week's performance to last week's performance, last month's performance to the month prior, and last month's performance to the same month the previous year.

2. Look at the charts over a long time frame.

Simply look at the charts over the longest time period possible and look for trends, without comparing date ranges. This approach is useful for a bird's eye view of the general direction your traffic is heading. This is not so effective for finding hard-to-find information or identifying granular insights, and you will be unable to compare specific percentages of moving trends.

Note: Seasonality is a factor affecting many businesses. Sometimes you may see a downturn in traffic, but this may not necessarily indicate your site is performing poorly. It could be your market experiences a downward trend in certain months. If your business is experiencing a downward trend, use the 'compare two date ranges' approach and compare the current month's traffic to the same month last year. If you are seeing increases, then you know your site is performing well, irrespective of seasonal trends.

Acquisition.

Acquisition is an area of Google Analytics any business owner or marketer should spend a lot of time reviewing. The Acquisition section of Google Analytics breaks down where your site traffic is coming from. Without keeping a close eye on your traffic sources, it is almost impossible to make informed judgments about the performance of your site or your marketing.

Click 'Acquisition' in the main sidebar on the left. In the 'All Traffic' section you can see actual amounts of traffic you've received from a given source. The Channels section listed under 'All Traffic' is of special interest. This lists the main sources sending customers to your website. From the 'channels' tab, you can dig further for deeper insights into the performance for specific sources sending customers to your site, such as social visitors, search engine visitors, email visitors, and so on.

Organic Search report

The Organic Search report is essential for monitoring your performance in search engines. Within the Organic Search report, you can actually see how many times you received a visitor from a search engine.

It's worth mentioning, a few years ago Google made changes to Google Analytics that still has many search engine marketers and marketing professionals shaking their fist at the sky. Early in 2012, Google changed this tool to hide a large portion of the keyword information, making it difficult to get exact information on the keywords customers are using. Thanks Google!

Now when someone types a phrase into Google, if they are signed into a Google account while browsing, the keyword the visitor searches for will show up as a 'not provided' keyword in Google Analytics report. When this happens, you have no idea what that person typed into Google before arriving at your site.

The amount of keyword information that has been obscured has gradually increased, but don't be too concerned, we can still measure overall performance of search engine traffic by looking for total increases or decreases in the Organic Search report.

To view the Organic Search report, click on the Acquisition tab on the left sidebar, click on 'All Traffic', click on 'Channels', and click on 'Organic Search'.

Segments.

Imagine if you could narrow down to a particular segment of your audience, such as paid traffic, search engine traffic, mobile traffic, iPad users, and so on, and instantly see how many enquiries these users have made, how much time they are spending on your site, what country they are from, and how many sales they are making. This feature exists and it is called Segments.

Segments are powerful. With Segments, you can identify portions of your audience that potentially generate more enquiries or sales than other customers. You can even identify portions of your audience having difficulty using your site, and get insights to fix these areas for better performance.

To use Segments, simply click on the 'Add Segment' tab at the top of every page within Google Analytics, and you can choose from the list a large number of Segments for deeper insights.

Common web analytics terms explained.

Pageviews.

A Pageview is counted each time a user loads a page on your site.

Unique Pageviews.

Similar to a Pageview, but if one user loads a page several times it will only be considered one Unique Pageview.

Session.

A session is what occurs when a visitor arrives at the site, and then at some point closes the browser. If that visitor returns again, this is counted as an additional session.

User.

If a user visits your site, and then returns at a later stage, this is counted as one unique User.

Bounce Rate.

If a visitor visits your site, and then leaves without visiting any more pages, this is a bounce. The percentage of visitors who bounce is your bounce rate. A common question among markets and business owners is: what is a good bounce rate? There is no general rule. Bounce rates vary greatly between sites and industries. If you find a particular page with a very high bounce rate (+70%), this could be an indicator the visitors do not like the content or they are experiencing technical issues.

Conversion rate.

One of the most important metrics to monitor is your site conversion rate. A conversion rate is the percentage of Users completing a desired action. The action could be filling out an enquiry form, downloading a product, or buying something from you. If you receive one hundred visitors, and three of these visitors complete a sale, this would be a three percent conversion rate.

Goals.

Goals are custom goals you can set up within Google Analytics to track particular business goals or targets you may have for your site.

Common goals to set up include newsletter signups, product downloads, enquiry form completions, and so on.

Other web analytics tools.

There are many web analytics tools out there to help with improving the performance of your site. Google Analytics is great for understanding overall traffic performance, but if you want to delve deeper, check out the following tools for greater insights:

Crazy Egg. Free to start. Starts at $108 per year for premium features. Requires a Google Account to get started.
http://www.crazyegg.com

If you want a visual indication of how visitors behave on your site once they arrive, Crazy Egg is a fantastic tool. With Crazy Egg, you can get heat maps of where visitors click on the page. You can also see heat maps of how far visitors scroll down the page.

Optimizely. Free for basic users.
http://www.optimizely.com

Optimizely is a popular split-testing analytics tool. With Optimizely you can split test different variations of your site, and see which version makes more sales or conversions.

Troubleshooting common SEO problems & how to fix them.

Dealing with Google can be massively frustrating at times. Customer support barely exists, and trying to understand why your site isn't playing well with Google can spiral into a wild goose chase.

Don't let Google's lack of customer support or the horror stories dishearten you. Most of the time, if a site is experiencing Google problems, it is only temporary. SEO problems are rarely irrecoverable.

Usually it's simply a matter of finding out the underlying cause of the problem — more often than not, the cause isn't what the popular blog posts are saying it might be. This sometimes means fixing several items. Once all fixed, you have stacked the deck in your favor and you are more likely to make a speedy recovery.

This chapter outlines common SEO problems that plague web site owners.

If you are not at all technically inclined, I urge you to read the section on getting additional advice, or even consider getting professional help if your site is experiencing serious SEO issues.

What to do when your site is not listed in Google at all.

This is a common problem among webmasters and business owners alike.

If you have just launched a brand new site, it is possible Google has not crawled your site yet. You can do a quick spot check by typing 'site:yoursiteaddress.com' into the Google search bar and checking to see if your site comes up at all. If it doesn't, it's possible Google's spider hasn't crawled your site and doesn't know it exists.

Typically all that's required for Google to pick up your site is to generate a handful of links to your site, and some social activity.

Tweeting a link to your site is a quick way to ensure your site is indexed by Google's software, typically within 24-hours. Try to share your site from a handful of social networks for faster results.

Check Google again in 24 hours with the 'site:www.yoursite...' search query and see if any pages from your site comes up. If you do see pages, this means Google has indexed your site.

If this doesn't work, ask your web designer to setup Google Webmaster Tools for you, login, and see if there are any errors. If there are errors, Google will outline the steps to fix them, so Google can see your site.

What to do when your business is not ranking for your own business name.

A business not coming up in the top position in Google for searches for the official business name is a surprisingly common issue among brand new sites. Google is smart, but sometimes you need to give Google a nudge to associate your new site with the name of your brand.

This solution is easily fixed by building links to your site, with some of the links with your brand name as the anchor text. This can take up to a couple of weeks for Google to see these links, connect the dots and realize your site is the real deal.

The fast way to get the ball rolling is to do a quick search for the business directories used in your country — Whitepages, Yellow Pages, Yelp, and so on — fill out a listing for your business on each site and include a link back to your web site. The more links the better, but you should be aiming for a minimum of 50 links. In 95% of cases, this will solve the problem of a site not coming up in the top results of searches for the business name.

If this doesn't work, setup Facebook and Twitter accounts for your business, filling out as much information about your business as possible in the profile. Then do a post a day for about two weeks, mixing in links to your site in the posts.

If you still can't get your site ranking high enough, use Open Site Explorer to spy on competing sites ranking higher for the brand name. Do their pages have more backlinks than the total amount of links to your site? If this is the case, you are going to need to build more links.

What to do when your rankings have dropped off.

Here's a sad truth about SEO: if you achieve a top ranking, it may not keep its position forever. There are billions of web pages competing for top positions in Google. New sites are being created every day. It requires an ongoing effort to keep pages ranking high.

If your rankings have dropped off from the top position, and are slowly moving their way down the search results, it's likely your competitors have simply acquired more links or more social activity. Use Open Site Explorer to spy on competitors, find out how many backlinks they have, how much social media activity they have, and set these amounts as your target to build your rankings back up.

Next, it's time to start a link building campaign with the targeted keywords as outlined in the chapter on link building.

If you are worried that you may have been penalized by the recent updates to Google, such as the Penguin update or the Panda update, read the next section for common recovery steps.

What to do when your site has been penalized by a Penguin update.

The recent updates to Google have many site owners worried. The media circus are partly to blame for this, but the controversy surrounding the Panda and Penguin updates created the misconception that most traffic issues are caused by these updates.

The real truth—these updates have affected a fraction of sites and these site owners are a very loud minority.

In most cases, if your rankings have dropped off, your competitors have simply acquired more 'SEO Juice' to their pages, and it's time to pick up your game. If your pages have moved down a few positions, refer to the above section on the steps to recovery.

If your rankings have completely disappeared from Google's top-30, and they were previously ranking in the top-10, then it is possible you may have been penalized from Google's Penguin update. Follow the below steps to confirm if this was the case and follow the recommended steps to make a recovery.

Read on with caution. Penalties from the Panda and Penguin updates are difficult to diagnose and even more difficult to heal. If you are out of your depth, you may need to seek professional help to make a speedy recovery.

1. Check Google Webmaster Tools.

Any site owners that have had a *manual* penalty imposed on Google will receive a notice like the one below. Log in to your Google Webmaster Tools account to see if you have received a notice like one of the examples below:

'Google Webmaster tools notice of detected unnatural links to....'

We've detected that some of your site's pages may be using techniques that are outside of Google's Webmaster Guidelines....'

If you have witnessed the above message in Google Webmaster tools, Google has placed a manual penalty on your site as a result of the new Google updates. If you do not see the above message, then it is unlikely you have received a manual penalty from Google.

2. Check your link profile.

Use Open Site Explorer, and Majestic SEO and look at the links pointing to the page you suspect may have been penalized. Do the same for the competing pages that are currently ranking in the top position for your keywords.

Look for the indicators below to confirm if your site has been penalized by the Google updates.

1. Your site has a much larger quantity of links than competitors, but isn't ranking in the top-50 for the same keyword.

If you have a significantly larger amount of links pointing to your page than competing sites, and your site is nowhere to be seen in the top-50 (but it was before), then you may have been penalized by the Penguin update.

2. Your site has a very large quantity of links from shoddy looking sites, e.g. sites that look like the following, seolinksdirectory.com, addurlsfree.com, freelinkdirectory.com, and so on.

3. Your page has anchor text pointing to the page for your targeted keyword greater than 20% as a general rule. Example: if 90% of the links pointing to the page have a targeted keyword as the anchor text, it is possible you may have been penalized by the Penguin update.

4. Use the Panguin tool to see if you have any sudden traffic declines around the times of the Google updates. If your traffic has not recovered, then it is possible your site has been penalized by Penguin.

Panguin tool
http://barracuda.digital/panguin-tool/
Google Penguin recovery steps

The following list walks you through the process required to heal a site penalized by Google Penguin. Please note, before you do any of these items, you must be absolutely confident your site has been affected by these updates. If your site has not been penalized by these updates, the below steps could do more harm than good to your site. If you are certain, it is highly recommended you seek professional advice.

1. Export all the backlinks to the page that has been penalized, using your Google Webmaster tools account, Open Site Explorer and Majestic SEO. Compile all of the links together into an Excel spreadsheet.

Go through and group together the links on spammy domains (e.g. freelinks.tv, seolinksdirectory.com, freeseolinks.com, bizlinks.biz and so on).

2. Visit each of these spammy sites and look for a link removal page. If there is no link removal page, find a contact page and request the site administrator to remove your link from their site. Provide a link to the page in your message to make it easier for the webmaster.

If you cannot locate any contact information for the site, use Domain Whois to find the site owner's contact details and contact the owner directly.

Domain Whois
http://whois.domaintools.com/

Document all of these efforts in a spreadsheet with a date, time and outcome.

3. After you have allowed one-to-two weeks for the webmasters to remove the links to your site, find the spammy links for the sites you have not been able to remove and put each of these bad links into a plain text file, with each link placed on a new line.

Log into Google Webmaster Tools and submit these links using the 'Remove URLs' page in the 'Optimization' section. Again, if you are uncertain about what you are doing, consult a professional SEO otherwise you could risk doing more harm than good.

4. File a reconsideration request in Google Webmaster tools. This should only occur after you have made a very thorough effort to remove your links manually and then disavowed the links through the disavow link tool.

You must submit a request to Google to let them know you believe you have been blocked by the Penguin update, and have gone to great efforts to clean up the link spam.

To do this, visit the following URL after logging into your webmaster tools account:

File a reconsideration request
https://www.google.com/webmasters/tools/reconsideration?pli=1

5. Await response and monitor rankings changes.

As mentioned, recovering from a Google Penguin penalty is not something anybody should do without a base level of professional SEO experience and complete confidence the site has been penalized by the Penguin update.

These steps have been included for those with SEO experience, and to illustrate the steps required to recover from a Penguin penalty.

It is highly recommended you speak with an expert before doing any of the above to attempt to recover from a penalty.

How to seek professional help for free.

Finding the right SEO help can be frustrating for site owners. There is a lot of information to navigate, with varying levels of quality and accuracy. It's difficult to get in touch with SEO practitioners at the top of their field.

That said, there are sites that can put your questions in front of world-leading experts of almost any topic for free. Use the below sites for highly technical responses, and you can create an army of Internet experts to try to solve your problem for you.

The key to success with the below resources is to be specific. The more specific you are, and the more information you provide, you increase your chances you will receive a detailed answer that will point you in the right direction.

For greater results, post your question on *all* of the sites below, and sit back and wait for the answers to come in. You will get more answers and will be in a better position to consider which solution is best.

MOZ Q&A
http://moz.com/community/q
MOZ's Q&A forums used to be private, but eventually recently released this feature open to the public. Here you can speak with a large number of SEO professionals directly and attract high quality answers to your questions. Great for SEO specific problems.

Pro Webmasters
http://webmasters.stackexchange.com

The Pro Webmasters Q&A board can have your questions answered by webmasters of high-performing sites.

Quora
http://www.quora.com
Quora is an all-round Q&A posting board, where you can get a question answered on almost anything. On Quora, questions are often answered by high-profile experts. Marketers, business owners, you name it, there are many leading industry authorities posting answers to questions on Quora.

Stack Overflow
http://stackoverflow.com

Created by the founders of Pro Webmasters, Stack Overflow is a community of web developers answering web development related questions. If you have a very technical question related to your site, or if you just want to keep your web developer honest by getting a second opinion, Stack Overflow is a great resource for getting highly technical questions answered.

Wordpress Answers
http://wordpress.stackexchange.com

If your site is built on Wordpress, it's inevitable you will eventually encounter some kind of technical hurdle. The Wordpress Answers Q&A board is a great resource to seek out help.

Indexing & SERP Display Problems and Questions
High Rankings Forum
http://www.highrankings.com/forum/index.php/forum/67-indexing-and-serp-display-problems-and-questions/

This discussion board on the High Rankings forum is specifically related to users having trouble getting their site to rank in Google. Here you will find answers for tough questions with a fast turnaround time. As is the case with all discussion boards, you can have a lively discussion about any topic, but you should always cross-reference and verify any information you receive.

Local SEO. SEO for local businesses.

Why use Local SEO?

Unless you have been living under a rock, you have seen listings for local business appearing at the top of some search results in Google. Local listings – previously known as Google Place page listings, now known as Google+ pages – are a great tool for local businesses looking to get more customers.

Local search results differ from traditional 'organic' search results, as they are a search engine result representing a local business, instead of a web page like normal search results.

Users can see business contact details at a glance, and find the information they need, instead of having to click through and dig around a clunky business site.

Local SEO can be a powerful tool to attract traffic. In many cases, local SEO can lead to many more inquiries for local businesses than regular SEO rankings.

Does this mean you should scrap traditional SEO in favor of local SEO? Nope. You can do both, and increase the amount of potential traffic your site can receive.

How to rank high with local SEO.

Ranking high with local SEO takes a much different approach than traditional SEO. Google's algorithm is looking for a different set of signals to determine the popularity of a business, to decide how high to rank it in the search results.

If you think about it, if a restaurant is really popular in a city, a whole bunch of links from sites all over the world probably isn't the best factor to determine how popular the business is in a local area.

A better indicator of the importance of a local business would be mentions of the business name and phone number, customer reviews, and the proximity of the business to the area being searched.

Below is a list of the most important ranking factors Google use for local listings:

1. Physical address in city of search.
2. Proper category associations (you must choose the most accurate category for your business).
3. Consistency of structured citations (amount of pages listing your business name and phone number correctly).
4. Quality/authority of structured citations (quality of the sites listing your business name and phone number).

5. Html NAP matching my business page nap (exact correct business details listed on business listings and website).
6. Product / service keyword in business title.
7. Domain authority of website (amount and quality of links pointing to web site).
8. Proximity of address to the point of search (searcher-business distance).
9. Individually owner-verified my business page.
10. Proximity of address to city centoid (location of business to center of city).

These are the strongest factors fetched from Moz's. If you want to rank high in the local search results, all you have to do is ensure your site and place page have more of these features than competitors ranking for your target keywords.

For a complete breakdown of the local SEO ranking factors, visit the below link, where one of the world's leading authorities on local SEO publish an industry survey on the local ranking factors every year.

Moz's Local Search Ranking Factors
https://moz.com/local-search-ranking-factors

Getting started with Local SEO.

To get started, the first step is to create your business page on Google+. Visit the URL below, and complete every area of your profile as possible. This means creating a detailed description of your business, uploading as many photos as you can, listing trading hours, payment methods you accept, and so on. The more information you complete in your profile, the more you increase your chances of Google ranking your page higher.

Google+ My Business
https://www.google.com/business

When creating your business listing, make sure you choose the correct category you want your business listing to appear in, e.g. if you provide plumbing as a service, you want to choose 'plumbing' as your category, not 'trades' or 'home repairs'.

Building citations.

Citations are the links of local SEO. A citation occurs each time your name, address, phone number (NAP) is mentioned on the web. The more citations you have than competitors, the more likely your site will rank higher than theirs. The easiest places to build citations are the many local business directories available for businesses.

Visit the below list from the LocalSEOGuide.com for a more comprehensive list of local business directories:

55 largest local business directories in the US
http://www.localseoguide.com/best-local-business-
directories-seo/

Building reviews.

Citations and reviews are the link building of local SEO. If you are only building citations, you only have half of the equation covered. To rank highly, you need to be aggressive in ensuring your business accumulates online reviews.

Many businesses struggle with this. This is because it's tough to get customers to fill out reviews!

You have to make it easy for your customers. Make it easy for your customers to fill out reviews and you will get more reviews.

Include links to your business Google+ page on your site, email signatures, flyers, and business cards, prompting customers to leave a review. Encourage customers at the end of each job or transaction to leave a review. By creating every opportunity possible for customers to leave a review, you will significantly increase the amount of reviews you receive.

But whatever you do, do not buy reviews. This is a quick way to get into Google's naughty books. Purchased reviews can be picked up by Google's filters and not included on the profile.

The new meta: Microformats, Microdata, schema.org & Facebook Open Graph.

Microformats, RDFa, microdata & schema.org. Where to start?

A growing problem has emerged on the Internet in the past couple of years. There's literally billions of sites and webpages with an infinite amount of information — all completely unorganized... A bureaucratic nightmare!

There are endless pages about movies, customer reviews, local businesses, product catalogs, and so on, and there has been no standardized way of organizing or presenting this information.

A need emerged for a universal method to make it easy for search engines to quickly recognize this information.

Hence the birth of 'meta data' or 'semantic data' markup —
new technologies that can be used on your site making it
easier for search engines — and other technologies — to
crawl, recognize and present your content to Internet
users.

Considering banging your head against the wall,
wondering why you're reading such a soul-destroyingly
dry topic? Well, don't throw this book out the window just
yet...

These new technologies mean you can have greater control
over your search listings, make it easier for search engines
to crawl your site, and achieve 'rich snippets' like the
example below, with which you can achieve higher click-
through-rates and get more eyeballs on your content.
Think of this new technology like meta description tags on
steriods.

Slipknot Tickets | Slipknot Concert Tickets & Tour Dates ...
www.ticketmaster.com › ... › Hard Rock/Metal ▾ Ticketmaster ▾
Results 1 - 10 of 21 - Buy Slipknot tickets from the official Ticketmaster.com site. Find
Slipknot tour schedule, concert details, reviews and photos.

Sat, Oct 25	KNOTFEST - SATURDAY ...	San Manuel Amphitheater ...
Sat, Oct 25	Knotfest - 2 Day Pass	San Manuel Amphitheater ...
Sun, Oct 26	KNOTFEST - SUNDAY Single ...	San Manuel Amphitheater ...

Why use schema.org

So now we know what we can do with this new technology, where do we start? As always with new technologies, there's an ongoing debate about the best to use — RDFa, microdata, hCards, microformats, the list goes on...

Well I won't waste your time with a technical debate. Google, Yahoo and Bing joined together in 2011 to hit the data nail on the head and created a standardized approach with schema.org — a reference site for the Microdata markup technology, which allows you to cover all of your meta-data needs.

Google openly stated Microdata, and it's sister-site schema.org, is their preferred technology, and made it clear not to mix 'meta data' technologies — fear of confusing their spider.

We're here for high rankings and traffic, not a lengthy diatribe on each individual technology, so let's go with what Google recommends for the purposes of this book.

How to use schema.org.

Google supports the below custom listings in the search results. If you have any of the below, your site can benefit from use of schema.org's recommended additional markup for your site.

- Reviews

- People
- Products
- Businesses and Organizations
- Recipes
- Events
- Music
- Video content

We'll use an example of a business listing to see how it might normally be coded, compared to following schema.org's recommendation.

Standard code for business details

```
<h1>Beachwalk Beachwear & Giftware</h1>
<p>A superb collection of fine gifts and clothing to accent
your stay in Mexico Beach.</p>
<p>3102 Highway 98</p>
<p>Mexico Beach, FL</p>
<p>Phone: 850-648-4200</p>
```

Microdata formatted code for business details

```
<div itemscope
itemtype="http://schema.org/LocalBusiness">
  <h1><span itemprop="name">Beachwalk Beachwear &
Giftware</span></h1>
  <span itemprop="description"> A superb collection of
fine gifts and clothing
  to accent your stay in Mexico Beach.</span>
  <div itemprop="address" itemscope
itemtype="http://schema.org/PostalAddress">
```

```
<span itemprop="streetAddress">3102 Highway
98</span>
<span itemprop="addressLocality">Mexico
Beach</span>,
<span itemprop="addressRegion">FL</span>
</div>
Phone: <span itemprop="telephone">850-648-
4200</span>
</div>
```

You can see how the above code gives the search engine a friendly nudge to recognize the information as a business listing, such as the address and the phone number.

While the above example will be just enough if you have a simple business listing, if you have any of the earlier-mentioned types of information on your site, you'll have to log on to schema.org to follow their documentation to ensure your data is correctly formatted.

Schema.org
http://schema.org

Facebook Open Graph.

While we know schema.org is the best approach for adding meta data to your site, there is one additional 'meta data' technology you should also use...

Facebook's Open Graph language allows you to determine how your site listing appears when shared on Facebook.

If you do not include Facebook's Open Graph code on your site, when a user shares your content on Facebook it will show a plain listing on the news feed, with the responsibility on the user to describe the article and make it worth reading. If you include Facebook Open Graph code, it comes up looking sexy, just like your search listings if you have been using your meta title and meta description tags correctly.

By putting your best foot forward, and making your listing show up correctly on Facebook, you will encourage more customers to click to your site, and increase the amount of likes and shares of your page. This will increase the social signals of the page.

Here's an example of properly formatted meta code using Facebook Open Graph. As you can see, there are only minor tweaks required to make your page show up nicely on Facebook's news feed... So go ahead and use it on your site!

```
<title>Buy Baseball Jackets Online</title>
<meta property='og:type' content='site'>
<meta property-'og:description' name='description' content='Wide range of Baseball Jackets online, for all leagues and players. Free delivery and free returns both-ways in USA.' />
```

If you're worried about confusing search engines by using several 'structured data' technologies at the same time, such as Open Graph and schema.org, don't worry, you won't have any problems.

Facebook Open Graph is mainly used by Facebook's web crawler, not by search engines, so you can use Open Graph and schema.org in tandem without any problems.

If you want to read up further on Facebook's Open Graph, or if you have complex types of listings on your site, checkout Facebook's Open Graph guide below.

Open Graph Protocol
http://ogp.me

Powerful SEO tools.

There are many powerful SEO tools that can help save hours, days, or even weeks of your time.

The following tools can help find link building opportunities, diagnose site issues, create easy-to-understand SEO reports, make Google crawl your site faster and much more. More often than not, the below tools will provide information you need to achieve high rankings, and reveal link building opportunities so you can go out and get those high rankings.

Are there more SEO tools out there than in this list? Sure. SEO tools are a dime a dozen. The following is a selection of the tools I have found useful over the years and the tools mentioned in this book for ease of reference. Some are free, some are paid, but most offer a free trial long enough to start optimizing your site. I have no affiliation with any of these sites, I've just listed tools that I find useful. So jump in and have fun.

Research tools.

Google Adwords Keyword Planner. Free.
http://www.google.com/intl/en/adwords/

The Google Adwords Keyword Planner has been mentioned several times throughout this book and for good reason. It's essential for every SEO project. With the Google Adwords Keyword Planner you can see how many times a keyword has been searched in Google and narrow this down by Country and even device type, such as mobile phones and so on. This is an essential tool for every SEO project for knowing how many times your keyword is being searched in Google.

Google Trends. Free.
http://www.google.com/trends/

Google Trends provides powerful stats of search trends over time. Great for seeing how your market performs overall, and how demand changes over time for your keywords.

Market Samurai. Free to start. $149 for pro users.
http://www.marketsamurai.com/

Market Samurai is one of those reliable tools that have been around in the SEO industry for many years.

The favorite keyword research tool of many SEO gurus, Market Samurai is powerful for generating ideas for keywords and analyzing keywords for competitiveness — so you can uncover keywords you can target for easy rankings.

Moz. Free and Paid.
http://moz.com/tools

No book on SEO would ever be complete without a mention of Moz. Moz offers keyword analysis, brand monitoring, rankings tracking, on-page SEO suggestions, search engine crawl tests, and much more. An essential toolbox for every SEO practitioner, from beginner to advanced.

SEOBook Keyword Analyzer. Free.
http://tools.seobook.com/general/keyword-density/

By simply entering the URL to any page on your site, you can see a chart of the most optimized keywords on the page. This is great for getting a visual indication of keywords search engines are likely to pick up on the page.

SEOQuake. Free.
http://www.seoquake.com/

The SEOQuake toolbar gives you a powerful set of stats for any site you visit, right within your browser.

SEOQuake also has a great option that gives you the important stats for pages ranking in Google's search results. A great tool for snooping on competitors and doing market research.

SEOQuake's powerful toolbar works on Google Chrome, Safari & Firefox.

Ubersuggest. Free.
http://ubersuggest.org/

Automatically download the auto-suggested keywords from Google's search results for a nice, juicy collection of long-tail keywords.

Optimization tools.

Google Page Speed Insights. Free.
https://developers.google.com/speed/pagespeed/insight
s

Google Page Speed Insights is a fantastic tool provided by Google to help speed up your site. Google Page Speed Insights will give you a score on how well your load time is performing, and provides a simple set of suggestions to forward to your developers and speed up your site.

Google Snippet Optimization Tool. Free.
http://www.seomofo.com/snippet-optimizer.html

This handy little tool lets you type out title tags and meta tags and see a live preview of how your site will appear in the search engines.

Google Webmaster Tools. Free
https://www.google.com/webmasters/tools/home?hl=e
n

Google Webmaster Tools is another great tool, and if you haven't got Google Webmaster Tools set up, drop what you are doing and set it up now!

Google Webmaster Tools will report urgent messages if there are any severe problems when Google comes along and crawls your site. You can also submit your sitemap directly to Google from within Webmaster Tools, meaning you know Google has been given a friendly nudge to come around and pick up all the content on your site. This is a must-have SEO tool for every site.

Redirect Checker. Free.
http://www.seologic.com/webmaster-tools/url-redirect

If you have ever setup a URL redirect — or asked your developer to — it's always a good idea to check and ensure the redirect has been setup correctly.

Use the redirect checker to make sure your redirects are returning successful responses to the web browser, so you can feel confident Google is picking it up properly too.

Robots.txt Analyzer. Free
http://tools.seobook.com/robots-txt/analyzer/

Many robots.txt files can often have slight errors that are difficult to pick up, especially for larger sites. Run your robots.txt file through this tool for a free analysis to see if there are any errors.

Robots.txt Generator. Free
http://www.yellowpipe.com/yis/tools/robots.txt/

If you're lazy like I am, you'll love this free robots.txt generator. Works great for the most basic or advanced robots.txt users to create robots.txt files quickly and easily.

Schema Creator. Free
http://schema-creator.org/

Great and easy-to-use tool to automatically generate your
schema.org markup.

SEO Browser. Free
http://seo-browser.com

Takes a webpage or site, and shows you what it looks like
to a search engine, without graphics and layout. This is a
fantastic tool for getting a birds eye view of what Google is
going to pick up on your site.

Tools Pingdom. Free.
http://tools.pingdom.com/fpt/

Pingdom search tools is a great tool for monitoring how
quickly your site is loading, and finding opportunities to
make it load even faster.

With the Pingdom Speed test you can see how fast your
site loads, and how large the files are on your site. You can
easily find the large files on your site that are chewing up
resources and bloating your load time.

Pingdom also offers a really nifty service to monitor your site uptime, and send you a text message and email alert whenever your server experiences problems and goes down for whatever reason. You can find out before anybody else and jump on your web hosting provider and ask them to fix any problems, before you lose too much traffic!

Traffic Travis. Free for beginners. $97 once off for Pro users.
http://www.traffictravis.com

Traffic Travis is a great and simple SEO overview tool. Unlike many of the other tools listed, Traffic Travis is a downloadable tool you must download to your desktop (PCs only!).

Traffic Travis provides SEO health checks, competitor analysis, ranking tracking, linkbuilding research, and much more.

Xenu's Link Sleuth. Free
http://home.snafu.de/tilman/xenulink.html

Don't be put off by the old-school design on the page that offers this very powerful SEO-tool for free.

Xenu's Link Sleuth is one of the most powerful SEO-tools available, that will crawl your entire site, or a list of links, and offer very powerful and juicy stats for each of your pages, such as stats on which pages have 404 errors, 301 redirects, server errors, title tags, meta desc tags, the list goes on! This tool has been around for years, and is a must-have tool for the more advanced SEO practitioner.

XML Sitemaps. Free to trial. $19.99 for large sites. http://www.xml-sitemaps.com

XML Sitemaps is a fantastic tool for creating an XML sitemap to submit to Google. Useful for sites that do not have a built in XML sitemap functionality.

The tool automatically formats the sitemap so it is in the right format for Google and other search engines. With XML Sitemaps you can create a sitemap for your site within minutes.

Link building tools.

Authority Labs. Free to start. $99 per month for pro users. http://authoritylabs.com/tour/

Authority Labs is a great tool for tracking your rankings in search engines. You can also track competitors' rankings too. Monitoring your rankings is a must for every SEO project, so you can measure improvements or trends over time.

Buzzstream. Free trial. $19 per month for regular use. http://www.buzzstream.com

Buzzstream helps you find broken linkbuilding opportunities and track your linkbuilding outreach efforts. Buzzstream will even find the contact details on the site for you. Can be used as an alternative to Ontolo.

Google Alerts. Free.
http://www.google.com/alerts

Google Alerts is great for keeping an eye out for fresh new search results in Google.

You can put in any search term, add your email address, and Google Alerts will send you an email each time a new listing appears in Google's search results.

Great for monitoring new links pointing to your site, mentions of your brand, new content indexed by Google, or even brand mentions of your competitors — so you can reach out and build links or add comments.

Majestic SEO Site Explorer. Free to start. £29.99 for pro plan.
https://majestic.com

Majestic SEO Site Explorer is a lesser known, but powerful link analysis tool.

Majestic's Site Explorer allows you to download historical reports of links built to a site, so you can see the historic patterns behind a site's link building.

Majestic SEO also has a very powerful tool called the Keyword Checker. The Keyword Checker allows you to analyze the competition for specific keywords, so you can know how difficult it will be to rank high enough for particular keywords.

Ontolo. $47 per month.
http://www.ontolo.com

Ontolo is a goldmine for broken link building, making it very easy to filter through many broken link opportunities, so you can reach out and start building links.

Open Site Explorer. Free for limited access. $99 per month for pro users.
https://moz.com/researchtools/ose/

Open Site Explorer is a must for understanding the links pointing to your site and competitors' sites. Cheeky little tricks with Open Site Explorer include exporting your competitors' backlinks and looking over these links for opportunities to build links to your site.

Everything You Need to Know About Penguin 2.0 & Hummingbird.

On May, 22nd, 2013 Google's head of web spam, Matt Cutts, announced the next big update affecting sites appearing in the search results. This update is called Penguin 2.0.

After Google's history of releasing game changing updates, this update had been anticipated, even feared, by many members of the SEO community.

And for good reason. The updates released in previous years caused entire sites to drop completely out of Google, and many webmasters and SEOs were forced to change their entire approach to marketing their business.

Here's what Matt Cutts posted on his blog:

We started rolling out the next generation of the Penguin webspam algorithm this afternoon (May 22, 2013), and the rollout is now complete. About 2.3% of English-US queries are affected to the degree that a regular user might notice. The change has also finished rolling out for other languages world-wide. The scope of Penguin varies by language, e.g. languages with more webspam will see more impact.

Why you should keep a cool head about Penguin 2.0

Penguin has been anticipated by Google and the SEO community as a game-changing update. However, many members of the SEO community haven't been affected by this update at all. Why is this so?

The update is a more widespread version of the first Penguin update. Bad practices that Penguin 1.0 and Penguin 2.0 penalizes, such as overly spammy anchor text, and links from low quality sites, have not been widely used or supported by the SEO community for the past 12-months.

This update is much more likely to affect very low quality, spam-related sites that are using outdated 'black-hat' tactics.

If you have been following the link building best practices outlined in this book, you can breathe a sigh of relief—it's unlikely you will have been negatively affected by this update.

What Does Penguin 2.0 Target?

Google never fully reveals the inner workings of their updates, otherwise Google would be making it easier for the evil spammers to fill up the search results with low-quality pages. That said, we can piece together reports from Google and the SEO Community to create a fairly clear picture of what this update targets.

Matt Cutts publicly said the Penguin 2.0 update is further devaluing web spam and suspicious links pointing to sites. So we know the update is focused on low-quality links.

An online study by the industry authority Search Engine Watch revealed sites affected by the Penguin 2.0 update typically had 66% targeted keywords in their links pointing to the page, while healthy sites in the top-10 had targeted keywords making up no more than 29% of the links pointing to a particular page. The lessons learned from the first Penguin update still remain true. Your target keyword text should not take up more than 20-30% of the links pointing to a page.

Google have also mentioned that this update should affect industries differently. The below study by Mozcast.com reveals how much the rankings have changed across the different industries. A higher temperature in the list indicates the rankings are moving around considerably.

The first temperature listed is the temperature (volatility) of the rankings after the update, and the second temperature is the volatility of the rankings before the update. A higher % change means the industry has been heavily affected by this update.

- 33.0% (80°/60°) – Retailers & Merchandise
- 31.2% (81°/62°) – Real Estate
- 30.8% (90°/69°) – Dining & Nightlife
- 29.1% (89°/69°) – Internet & Telecom
- 26.0% (82°/65°) – Law & Government
- 24.4% (79°/64°) – Finance
- 23.5% (81°/65°) – Occasions & Gifts
- 20.8% (88°/73°) – Beauty & Personal Care
- 17.3% (70°/60°) – Travel & Tourism
- 15.7% (87°/75°) – Vehicles
- 15.5% (84°/73°) – Arts & Entertainment
- 15.4% (72°/62°) – Health
- 15.0% (83°/72°) – Home & Garden
- 14.2% (78°/69°) – Family & Community
- 13.4% (79°/70°) – Apparel
- 13.1% (78°/69°) – Hobbies & Leisure
- 12.0% (74°/66°) – Jobs & Education
- 11.5% (88°/79°) – Sports & Fitness
- 7.8% (75°/70°) – Food & Groceries
- -3.7% (70°/73°) – Computers & Electronics

What to do about Penguin 2.0?

Whatever you do, don't lose your mind and start making drastic changes on your site. It's very likely your site weathered the storm, or if you have noticed some slight changes — it's also likely you are experiencing normal ranking movements.

If you are concerned or have reason to believe your site has been affected by this update, progress through the following steps and you can identify the cause and make appropriate action steps:

1. Check your rankings and traffic around the 20th of May, 2012. Have you noticed any clear decreases in traffic, visits from particular keywords, or movement in rankings?

2. If you have noticed any of these decreases, identify the pages that will have been affected, and look up the pages' back-link information in Open Site Explorer (https://moz.com/researchtools/ose/) or Majestic SEO (https://majestic.com). Do these pages have suspicious amounts of over-optimized, saturated anchor text pointing to the page, or a large amount of low quality sites linking to the page?

3. If you have noticed a decrease around the 22nd of May, 2012 and have confirmed there are spammy links pointing to the page, follow the steps in the chapter on troubleshooting common SEO problems. The steps are the same for Penguin 2.0 penalties.

If your site is not showing any of the above warning signs, it's likely you have weathered the storm.

What you need to know about the Hummingbird update.

With a habit of surprising search engine marketers and businesses with gigantic updates, on September 26th 2013, Google announced the biggest update to their core algorithm.

Titled 'Hummingbird', this major update was a total overhaul of Google's algorithm that determines which search results are the most relevant to the user. This update focused on improving the ability for the algorithm to better understand the intent behind a user's search. Google's talented technical gurus achieved this by improving the technology that understands the contextual terms in a search query.

For example, if you searched for 'where to buy an iPhone 5', which this new algorithm Google should be able to understand you're looking for a location near your home to buy an iPhone.

Google search chief Amit Singhal stated 'Hummingbird is the first major update of it's type since 2001'. At the same conference, Matt Cutts reported that Google was using the algorithm for a month before it was even announced, and no-one even noticed!

So you might be wondering how this affects you...

Keep on creating the best, highest-quality content as you should be already. Make your pages relevant to the user. This was not an update targeting link building or spammers. With the Hummingbird update, it's business as usual.

Bonus chapter: Google's 2014 & 2015 algorithm updates.

Some might say the 2014 and 2015 Google algorithm updates were less severe than previous years. Recent Google updates largely affected large brands or sites using extremely spammy SEO tactics.

That said, if you want to be successful, you need to be well-informed on the latest updates to ensure your site doesn't trigger Google's spam filters. In some cases, you can take advantage of updates to the algorithm and get higher rankings.

Listed below are recent major updates to be aware of:

Panda 4.0.

On May 20, 2014, Matt Cutts, the head of Google's web spam team — the team that release the majority of updates to Google's algorithm — confirmed Google was rolling out another major update.

Reports from SEO professionals and webmasters confirmed this was an update targeting large sites and brands using scraped or copied content. Sites such as ask.com and ebay.com are examples of sites affected. These sites were penalized for the below areas:

- Poor user experience.
- Scraped content.

The above definitions are somewhat vague, making it hard to confirm if affected by the Panda update. To identify a Panda penalty, below are some questions to ask:

- Is there a visible drop-off in search engine traffic starting around late May, 2014?
- Does my site scrape large amounts of content from other sites?
- Does my site create a large amount of pages with duplicate content, or pages with light content, creating a poor user experience?

If the answer to all questions is no, give yourself a pat on the back. You have nothing to worry about.

If the answer to any of the above is yes, the below excerpt by one of the leading bloggers covering Panda 4.0, Glenn Gabe, sums it up nicely, or not so nicely if you've been a victim...

"If you anger users, provide a horrible user experience, present low-quality content, or deceive them in any way, the mighty Panda may pounce. Google can pick up when users are unhappy, and if that happens enough, you could be heading down a very dangerous path Panda-wise."

While there is no official guideline from Google on how to recover from a Panda penalty, below is a straightforward treatment plan if visibly affected and need to work on recovering your rankings.

Please note: Only proceed through the below if it is very clear you've been affected by this update. It is recommended you confirm with an experienced SEO professional before proceeding with any of the below steps:

- Remove any widgets or scripts using scraped content.
- Delete any sections with a high amount of duplicated content.
- Alternatively, use no-index and no-follow meta tags to block sections filled with duplicate content from search engines. Or use rel=canonical tags on duplicate pages to point search engines to the original page.
- If you have a large amount of ads pushing your content below-the-fold, you may have to rearrange the ads on your site so your content appears above-the-fold, and you provide a more positive experience for users.

Authorship Photo Drop.

You may remember Google+ profile photos appearing alongside articles and listings in the Google search results. Now these listings have become a relic of the past.

On June 26th, 2014, Google's trends analyst, John Mueller, announced to the world that Google will remove all author photos and Google+ view and subscriber counts from the Google search results, with the aim of providing a more consistent experience across devices.

Shortly after the photos were dropped from the search results, with the exception of the 'Google News' search results.

Does this mean you shouldn't be making use of Google's authorship by linking up your Google+ profile with content or articles you publish online?

Not necessarily. While the photos no longer appear in the results, ranking factors have not been affected by this update.

In fact, if you are regularly publishing blog posts or articles, you should verify your authorship with your Google+ account following the instructions from the below article. This will allow you to take advantage of the positive ranking factors resulting from verified authorship.

Author Information in Search Results
https://support.google.com/webmasters/answer/140898
6

Pigeon.

On July 24th, 2014, Google confirmed the release of a new algorithm update called 'Pigeon', sending the SEO community into a flutter...

This was an algorithmic update, and not a penalty-based update, targeting local search results. This means no penalties were introduced. What was affected were parts of Google's algorithm that determine how local listings appear high or low, and how often the local listings appear at all.

The three major impacts of this update are listed below, with suggestions on what to do if you have been affected:

1) Local rankings are increasingly affected by domain authority.

Suggestion: If you have local listings in Google and noticed a decrease in ranking position, it's time to start working on building the amount of quality links pointing to your site.

2) Local listings disappearing for a large amount of keywords.

Suggestion: If you were depending on local search results, and the local results are no longer showing up for your keywords, start working on acquiring organic non-local rankings, and maybe even considering a pay-per-click campaign while you are waiting for your new rankings to build up.

3) Large directories such as Yelp, Urbanspoon, Tripadvisor and Booking.com receiving higher rankings.

Suggestion: If your competitors' listings on these major directories are ranking for your local keywords, you may want to confirm your existing lists on the major business directories. You may even want to consider building links to your directory listing to overtake your competitors' positions.

This update has been considered a major update, but like the earlier Panda update this year, many honest businesses have coasted through unscathed, which is a relief.

HTTPS/SSL update.

On August 26th, 2014, Google confirmed they started using HTTPS as a ranking signal. Albeit a minor signal, affecting less than 1% of searches.... For now.

Google openly admitted this is part of a long-term initiative to encourage the majority of site-owners to move over to using SSL to secure their sites.

Words on this straight from the horse's mouth:

"Over time, we may decide to strengthen it, because we'd like to encourage all site owners to switch from HTTP to HTTPS to keep everyone safe on the web."

From 'HTTPS as a ranking signal' - Google Webmaster Central Blog
http://googlewebmastercentral.blogspot.com/2014/08/https-as-ranking-signal.html

Does this mean you should rush out and change your entire site to HTTPS right now?

Not necessarily...

Migrating or reconfiguring your site address is a substantial undertaking, and only recommended for experienced SEO professionals and web developers.

Google may be considering making HTTP a stronger ranking factor in the future — but they haven't done it yet.

If you administer a large site, it may be worth speaking with your developer on what's required to install an SSL certificate on your site, so you can begin planning the infrastructure required to make this happen in future.

If you do move your site across to use HTTPS as the default method of accessing your site, you and your developer should read the below guide by Google in detail before making any changes:

Move A Site With URL Changes

https://support.google.com/webmasters/answer/603308
5?hl=en&ref_topic=6033084

Panda 4.1.

On September 23rd, 2014, Google announced another major
release to the Panda update, targeting pages with a poor
user experience, or pages with thin or extremely poor
content.

Like all Google updates, Google's description is painfully
vague and mysterious. Thankfully, the SEO community
have analyzed this update at great length and detailed
their findings online.

Sites negatively affected by this update:
- Sites extremely thin or light content, such as pages with
blank or empty content.
- Pages loaded with a large amount of affiliate links stuffed
into the content.
- Pages with a large amount of keyword stuffing on the
page.
- Pages with deceptive ad tactics, such as text link ads used
in key navigation areas in order to 'trick users' to click on
the ads.

In other words, pages that create a horrible experience for
users have been affected. The type of pages Google
obviously doesn't want ranking at the top of search.

This update is actually a blessing in disguise. Many site owners reported seeing a rise in rankings and traffic after the release of the update. Google themselves reported this update will result in many small to medium sites with good quality content rising to the top.

It's likely you haven't been impacted by this update if you haven't been using the tactics above. If you can see obvious changes in rankings or traffic around September 23rd, 2014, you may want to start focusing on improving the quality of the pages on your site.

Penguin 3.0.

On Friday, October 17th, 2014, Google announced the latest algorithm refresh titled 'Penguin 3.0'.

Like previous Penguin updates, this update is focused on low-quality links. This update is also focused on relieving penalties for site owners who cleaned up their low-quality link building in the past, and submitted a reconsideration request to Google.

At the writing of this book, there are few specifics published, besides Google stating it targets 'poor quality links'. As always, Google are tight-lipped with the details on how their algorithm works.

The good news is, overall, very few webmasters reported any issues. Look over your rankings and search traffic around October 17th, 2014. If you can't see any obvious trends, then it's likely you haven't been affected. If you notice any steep declines in rankings, or traffic around this date, then it's possible you have been affected and should look into it further.

If you have been creating high-quality links, and stayed away from spammy tactics like keyword stuffing, articles written in poor English, or spammy links built on low-quality sites, give yourself a cocktail and a pat on the back — there's nothing to worry about and it's time to get back to getting more rankings.

Key areas of note
- Penguin 3.0 is a worldwide refresh, affecting all countries.
- The refresh started rolling out from October, 17th, 2014.
- Impacts less than 1% of English queries.
- Pierre Far from Google specified this is a 'refresh' not an update. Historically, refreshes are less severe and affect fewer sites.

If you're a resource junkie, and dying to read up further, the below guide is a good summary:

Penguin 3.0: The Definitive Guide to Diagnosis and Recovery
http://www.forbes.com/sites/jaysondemers/2014/10/20/penguin-3-0-the-definitive-guide-to-diagnosis-and-recovery/

Doorway Pages.

In mid-March, 2015, Google announced their intent to release an update targeting 'doorway pages' in just a couple of weeks. Before I go into what doorway pages are, and how this update affects SEO practitioners, let's look at guidelines announced directly by Google on their webmaster blog. Their wording is somewhat vague, but don't be overwhelmed, I will explain how to avoid being affected in the following paragraphs.

"Here are questions to ask of pages that could be seen as doorway pages:

• Is the purpose to optimize for search engines and funnel visitors into the actual usable or relevant portion of your site, or are they an integral part of your site's user experience?
• Are the pages intended to rank on generic terms yet the content presented on the page is very specific?
• Do the pages duplicate useful aggregations of items (locations, products, etc.) that already exist on the site for the purpose of capturing more search traffic?
• Are these pages made solely for drawing affiliate traffic and sending users along without creating unique value in content or functionality?
• Do these pages exist as an 'island?' Are they difficult or impossible to navigate to from other parts of your site? Are links to such pages from other pages within the site or network of sites created just for search engines?"

An Update on Doorway Pages
http://googlewebmastercentral.blogspot.com/2015/03/a
n-update-on-doorway-pages.html

Doorway pages are essentially low-quality pages, created
with the sole intention of increasing rankings in Google,
that then funnel users into other actual useful areas of the
site.

It's an old-school, black-hat technique sometimes effective
for increasing traffic — that is, until Google put an end to it.

A red flag for this tactic is proactively building pages for
search engines, but keeping these pages hidden from
users. Another red flag is advertising affiliate offers (a.k.a
selling someone else's product for a commission) without
creating real value or content for the user beforehand.
Steer clear of these two red flags and you will be
unaffected by the Doorway Pages update.

To be clear, if your site has a directory structure with
multiple pages for cities or service areas, this is fine as long
as the pages offer unique and valuable content for uses,
such as; unique content, rich text and images, maps or
videos.

Mobile SEO update.

In early 2015, Google announced a game changing update for the SEO industry. As of April 21, 2015, sites with solid mobile support will rank higher in search results for mobile users. Sites with no mobile support will not rank highly in mobile search results.

Whether we like it or not, mobile users are here to stay. And whether we like it or not, Google is driving the mobile revolution. With the largest mobile app store in the world, the largest mobile operating system in the world, and the largest amount of mobile search users, it's easy to see why mobile users are a priority for Google.

Google is rolling out this update to give webmasters a nudge to make the Internet more user-friendly for mobile users. If you are not supporting mobile users, it's time to start seriously thinking about increasing your mobile support, not only for better search engine results, but for better sales and conversions — it's likely a very large segment of your traffic are mobile users.

If you are concerned about your rankings for searches performed on desktop and laptop machines you have nothing to worry about. Google has made it very clear this mobile friendly update will only affect search results on mobile devices.

What to do about the mobile update.

If you want to increase your support for mobile devices and be more search engine friendly, you have three options:

1. Create a responsive site.

Responsive sites are the cream of the crop when it comes to sites that support both desktop and mobile devices. With responsive sites, both mobile and desktop users see the same pages and same content, and everything is automatically sized to fit the screen. It's becoming more and more common for WordPress templates and new sites to feature a responsive layout.

2. Dynamically serve different content to mobile and desktop users.

You can ask your web developer to detect which devices are accessing your site and automatically deliver a different version of your site catered to the device. This is a more complicated setup, better suited for very large sites with thousands of pages, when a responsive approach is not possible.

3. Host your mobile content on a separate subdomain, e.g. m.yoursite.com

While Google have stated they support this implementation, I recommend against it. You need a lot of redirects in place, and must jump through giant hoops to ensure search engines are recognizing your special mobile subdomain as a copy of your main site. Responsive sites are popular for good reason: it's much easier and cheaper to maintain one site rather than additionally maintaining a mobile copy of your site on a mobile subdomain.

Google have stated that this mobile update is going to be fairly straightforward. Either your site supports mobile devices or it doesn't. Google will not reward sites with better mobile support with higher rankings over sites with average mobile support — for now. If your site supports mobile devices, you can rest assured you will most likely be fine with this update. Run your site quickly through the below tool and see if your site supports mobile devices in Google's eyes...

Mobile Friendly Test Tool
https://www.google.com/webmasters/tools/mobile-friendly/

The technical details of building a responsive site are beyond the scope of this book and could fill an entire book. That said, mobile SEO can be ridiculously simple.

If you have a responsive site that delivers the same content to mobile and desktop users, automatically resizes content to the screen, and is user-friendly, all you have to do is follow the SEO recommendations in this book, and your mobile results will be top notch from an SEO perspective.

For guidelines direct from the horse's mouth, so to speak, you can read Google's mobile support documentation for webmasters and web developers.

Mobile Friendly Sites
https://developers.google.com/webmasters/mobile-sites/

Finding More Mobile Friendly Search Results
http://googlewebmastercentral.blogspot.com/2015/02/finding-more-mobile-friendly-search.html

Google Phantom II / Quality Update.

At the beginning of May, 2015, many webmasters and SEO professionals noticed a shakeup in the search results, which has been labeled the 'Phantom II' update or 'Quality Update'. What they saw was a noticeable drop-off, or increase, in large websites, of anywhere up to 10%-20% in traffic.

While Google initially denied any changes, the SEO community dug around and confirmed the update with Google and that it affected large sites with significant page quality problems. Specifically, the update was a change to how Google assesses the quality of pages, and then subsequently lowers or increases their rankings accordingly.

If this sounds overwhelming, don't be worried — small businesses and blogs were largely unaffected. This website targeted large sites with significant amounts of user-generated content, or aggregated content. Examples include 'how-to' type websites, large directories, click-bait type sites, or social media sites.

Among sites negatively affected, there's a surprisingly small list of quality issues they have in common:

- Aggressive ads occupying the majority of screen real estate, above-the-fold.
- Duplicate content or pages, containing information lifted from other websites.
- Thin or light content, such as pages with only a few sentences.
- Poor quality content, such as pages littered with spelling mistakes and poor legibility.
- Pages with large amounts of low-quality, spammy user submitted comments.

Examples of sites hit with a decrease from this update include ehow.com, hubpages.com, rottentomatoes.com, and answers.com.

The sites affected have lots of user-generated pages, low-quality content, pages with content copied from other sites, and aggressive advertising techniques, and so on.

With this update, we can see quality is continuing to be a high-priority for Google and we should be providing a high-quality user experience for all visitors. Provide legible, unique, and good-quality content, and you are unlikely to run afoul of a Google quality update.

Panda 4.2 refresh.

Late July, 2015 Google confirmed a Panda 'refresh' is slowly rolling out over several months. Both the SEO community and Google have been tight-lipped about Panda 4.2. This is due to Google's slow rollout of this change, Google are releasing this update in increments spanning several months, making it extremely difficult to pick up exact changes to the algorithm.

Panda 4.2 is a refresh, not an update.

The exact terminology Google are using for Panda 4.2 is that it is a 'refresh', not an 'update'. This means Google are only making small tweaks to the Panda part of the algorithm that picks up web pages with low-quality content. It also means sites previously hit with a Panda penalty will likely have the penalty lifted if they have removed the cause of the penalty (typically thin or low-quality content being causes of a Panda penalty).

Sites affected by Panda 4.2.

This refresh will only affect about 2-3% of searches. The previous panda refresh affected 3-5% of searches in September, 2014, and the early Panda update in May, 2014 affected 7% of searches. This update only affects a fraction of sites compared to previous Panda updates.

If your site is a large directory, ecommerce retailer, publisher, affiliate site or blog, it may be a good idea to quickly look over your content quality and page templates for any obvious Panda penalty triggers. Examples include:

-        Duplicate pages or content.
-        Scraped content.
-        Pages with thin or low-quality content.
-        Aggressive ads above-the-fold or ads hidden in content.
-        Aggressive popups or deceptive user redirects.

If you don't have any obvious content quality issues, it's likely you won't be affected by Panda 4.2. As mentioned, Panda 4.2 is a refresh, not an update, meaning only small changes will be witnessed, and you should only concern yourself with Panda 4.2 if you are guilty of any of the above areas in your site.

Keep up to date with Google's 2015 updates.

As of the last couple of years, Google updates have become progressively frequent, with a change to the algorithm witnessed and reported every month or so. While I understand if the constant changes by Google make you feel like banging your head against the wall, don't be disheartened. It can be easy to keep up with the updates. The below resources are great for keeping your ear to the ground. If there is a significant update to Google's algorithm, it will be covered on at least one of the below pages:

Google Algorithm Change History
http://moz.com/google-algorithm-change

Google Webmaster Central Blog
http://googlewebmastercentral.blogspot.com

Google PageRank & Algorithm Updates
https://www.seroundtable.com/category/google-updates

Google's 2016 updates — what's on the horizon?

You don't need a crystal ball or secret informer at Google to get a general sense of what may be on the horizon. After reviewing a decade of updates made to Google's search algorithm, it's easy to get a solid idea of what changes Google is likely to make, before they roll out.

Before we take a look at what's coming up, let's look at something previous Google algorithm updates have in common. Almost all previous updates can give us insights into upcoming updates. Previous updates generally focus on two things; 1) filtering out spam and low quality websites, and 2) making the Internet and Google a better user experience. To figure out what Google may be working on, we should look at possible changes with these qualities.

1. Google further rewards secure sites.

Google has already publicly admitted user privacy and security are becoming an increasing area of focus. After the HTTPS update rewarding websites secured with SSL certificates in 2014, it makes sense for Google to continue this trend, and give more website owners a nudge to improve user security, perhaps increasing the boost SSL-secured sites receive in search results.

2. Further Penguin and Panda updates.

Penguin updates are generally those made by Google focused on link quality. Panda updates are typically focused on content quality. A solid update or refresh for each of these areas usually happens once every year. It's likely Google will improve its accuracy in finding low-quality, non-relevant spammy type links, and further devalue their power, in a Penguin update. Google may also make a further Panda update devaluing websites with low-quality content, scraped content, or over aggressive ads.

3. Google targets 'bad neighborhood' type sites.

As more traditional businesses move online, leading to increased pressure on Google from commercial advertisers, we may begin to see fewer results for sites perceived as part of a 'bad neighborhood' type network showing up in search. This includes sites advocating user privacy such as sites streaming illegal versions of TV shows and movies. Authoritative brands with large social audiences and brand recognition may continue to be rewarded with higher positions.

4. More mobile updates.

Google has spearheaded a very large 'pro-mobile' initiative in 2015 and in 2016 this is likely to continue, with mobile Internet usage expected to surpass desktop in 2016. Google's mobile index is separate to its desktop index, meaning mobile users are seeing different results pages than desktop users. Now Google have specialized their focus on mobile users, this will be optimized and improved. Expect more severe impacts on sites that don't support mobile, or more sophisticated algorithms for assessing how 'mobile friendly' a website really is.

5. Google search result layout changes.

Google continually makes small adjustments to how its search results appear to make Google more useful. Potential layout changes to results pages include better listings for mobile apps, more detailed listings for local businesses, and better support for listings using structured data markup such as schema.org. We may also see improvements to results for direct question type searches, such as FAQs and how-to type searches, as mobile users increase, Google will improve their support for mobile users needing information on-the-go.

That covers probable areas of focus for Google over the next 12-months, based on current online trends, and what many industry insiders believe are pending changes.

I don't have a crystal ball, and cannot see into the future — the above are just educated guesses. Don't run out and change your whole business based on speculation. That said, keep these areas in the back of your mind, so you don't get caught with your pants down from a Google update.

Focus on improving the quality of your site, provide good mobile support, and earn good quality backlinks and social media activity. If you focus on these areas, it's unlikely you will run into any major problems, and you will increase your online performance at the same time.

Bonus chapter: The quick and dirty guide to pay-per-click advertising with Google AdWords.

Why bother with pay-per-click advertising?

You would have to be as crazy as a box of weasels to pay each time someone visits your site with pay-per-click advertising, when you can rank high in Google for free... Right?

Not necessarily.

Pay-per-click advertising has certain advantages over SEO.

With pay-per-click you can:

- Send customers to your site within hours, not the months it sometimes takes for solid SEO results.

- Track results down to the penny, and get very clear insights into the financial performance of your advertising. Simply set up conversion tracking with the instructions provided by Google, or whichever pay-per-click provider you choose.
- Achieve a much larger overall number of customers to your site by running pay-per-click in tandem with your other marketing efforts.
- Achieve a positive financial return on your marketing spend in many cases, and keep on selling to these customers in the future.

There is one caveat to the last point.

If you are a small fish trying to enter an extremely competitive market, such as house loans, insurance or international plane flights, it's likely the big players in the market are buying a large amount of advertising, forcing the average cost-per-click to astronomical prices, and making it difficult for new players to get a profitable return...

If you're selling pizza delivery in New York, pool cleaning in Los Angeles, or cheap baseball jackets... In other words, if you're selling a common local trade, service, or product online, it's likely you can receive a profitable return on your advertising spend.

While pay-per-click really deserves its own book, this is a quick and dirty bonus chapter, jam-packed with just enough information to get a pay-per-click campaign setup, avoid common mistakes newbies make, and send more customers and sales to your business.

If you want to delve deeper into the science of pay-per-click advertising, I've included some great resources on AdWords at the end of the chapter.

Sound good? Let's get started.

Which is the best PPC provider to start with?

There are many pay-per-click providers out there, Google AdWords and BingAds are just two.

Google AdWords is generally the best starting point. You can sell anything on Google AdWords if you have money to spend because the user base is so large.

If you're looking to jump into pay-per-click advertising, get started with Google AdWords. Move on to the other pay-per-click networks after you have some experience under your belt.

Here's why AdWords is probably the best choice for your first foray into pay-per-click advertising:

- Fast, instant results. Send new customers to your site within an hour or two.
- Advanced targeting technology. Target users based on where they are located, or what browser or device they are using. Google's ad targeting technology is among the best in the world.

- With Google's search engine market share at 67%, and Bing at 18.7%, you can reach out to the largest potential amount of customers with Google.
- Due to the popularity of AdWords, there's a wealth of knowledge on running AdWords campaigns successfully.

Ensuring success with research and a plan.

Like all marketing projects, for an AdWords campaign to be successful, you need to start with research and a solid plan. Without first defining your goals, and designing a robust strategy to achieve them, it's impossible to create a successful marketing campaign — you'll have no way of determining if the outcome is successful!

Here are some important questions to ask yourself before you get started:

- What is the objective of the campaign? Sales, web enquiries, sign-ups, or branding?
- What is the maximum monthly budget you can afford?
- What is the maximum cost-per-enquiry, or cost-per-sale you can afford? For example, if you are selling snow jackets at $100, and your profit margin is 20%... You really can't afford to spend much more than $20 on each customer you acquire. Write this figure down, and review it later. You may need to first run a small test campaign to determine if pay-per-click is profitable, and the right marketing channel for your business.

- What are the most common characteristics of your customers? For example, if you're selling late-night pizza delivery in New York, you don't want to be paying for the lovely folk in Idaho searching for late-night pizza delivery. Write down your customers' common characteristics, and later in the settings recommendations, if there's an option to target these customers, I'll tell you how to do it.

How to choose the right kind of keywords.

It's the moment you've been waiting for. The keywords! Precious keywords.

Just like SEO, getting your keywords right with AdWords is critical if you want a successful campaign.

Unlike SEO, with AdWords there are different types of keywords, called keyword match-types. I've listed the main keyword match types below.

Broad match keywords.

The default type of keywords all AdWords campaign use – if you don't change any settings – are broad match keywords. With broad match keywords, Google will take any word out of your phrase, and serve up ads for searches hardly related to your phrase.

Needless to say, almost all new campaigns should NOT be using broad match keywords to start with. Have a look at the example below.

keyword:
tennis shoes

will trigger ads for:
designer shoes
dress shoes
basketball shoes
tennis bags
tennis equipment

Phrase match keywords.

Phrase match keywords will only show your ad for searches containing your core phrase. With phrase match keywords, you can exercise a higher level of control and purchase traffic from more relevant customers. And higher relevancy usually means more sales.

To enter a phrase match keyword, when adding keywords to your account, wrap the keywords with "" quotation marks and these keywords will become broad match keywords.

keyword:
"tennis shoes"

will trigger ads for:
tennis shoes
best tennis shoes
tennis shoes online

will not trigger ads for:

shoes tennis
tennis shoe
tennis sneakers
tennis players

Exact match keywords.

Exact match keywords will only trigger ads for the exact phrase you enter. Needless to say, with exact match keywords in your campaign, you can have a high level of accuracy, and achieve more sales. Exact match keywords are indispensable for every AdWords campaign.

To enter exact match keywords, wrap the keywords with [] brackets when adding keywords to your account, they will become exact match keywords.

keyword:
[tennis shoes]

will trigger ads for:
tennis shoes

will not match for:
tennis shoe
tennis shoes online
best tennis shoes

Broad match modified keywords.

Broad match modified keywords are a special keywords allowing you to have both accuracy and a large amount of exposure. With broad match modified keywords, you will trigger ads that include a combination of all of the words in your phrase.

To create broad match modified keywords, add a + sign to the keywords when adding them to your account.

keyword:
+tennis +shoes

will match for:
where to buy tennis shoes online
tennis shoes
buy shoes for tennis
buy tennis shoes

will not match for:
tennis joggers
buy tennis shoe
margaret thatcher

Negative keywords.

One of the most important, but easily overlooked keywords are negative keywords. Negative keywords will prevent your ads from showing for searches that include your negative keyword.

If you are using phrase match or any kind of broad match keyword, you should be using negative keywords. Negative keywords are vital for ensuring you are not paying for advertising for irrelevant searches.

Enter negative keywords in your campaign by adding a - minus sign in front of your keywords when adding keywords, or going to the 'shared library' on the left hand column in your AdWords account, and you can apply negative keywords across your entire account, a great time-saving tip.

keywords:
+car +service
-guide
-manual

will trigger ads for:
car service los angeles
car service mechanic
car service tips

will not trigger ads for:
free car service guide
ford mustang 65 car service manual

When choosing keywords, you need a balance between keywords with a high level of accuracy, such as exact match keywords, and keywords with a larger amount of reach, such as phrase match or broad match modified keywords.

Use a mix of the above keywords in your campaign, then review the performance of different keyword types after your campaign has been running, when you have some data.

Structuring your campaign with ad groups.

AdWords offer an excellent way of organizing your keywords called ad groups.

If you organize your campaign correctly, you can quickly see which areas of your campaign are profitable and not-so-profitable.

Fortunately, AdWords offers a very powerful way to structure your campaigns called ad groups.

Let's say you have a Harley Davidson dealership, with a wide range of HD gear from bikes to accessories and clothing, below is an example of ad groups you might create

- Harley Davidson motorbikes
- Harley Davidson parts
- Harley Davidson accessories
- Harley Davidson jackets

With ad groups you can:

- Create separate ads from the rest of your campaign. Great for testing.

- Have a select range of keywords, specific to the ad group.
- Set a specific bid for the ad group. Great if you have higher-priced products or services you're willing to pay more for.
- Get detailed data on the performance of your ad groups.

Structure your campaign with ad groups with a very clear and simple sense of organization when you setup your AdWords campaign. You'll get better insights into the performance of your campaign, and it will make your life easier when you want to make changes later on down-the-track.

How to crush the competition with killer AdWords ads.

Writing a killer AdWords ad is essential to the success of your campaign. Poorly written AdWords ads can increase the overall costs of your campaign, sending less traffic to your site for more money.... We don't want that.

With your AdWords ads, you want to:

- Attract clicks from interested customers, not tire-kickers.
- Include keywords related to what the user searched for.
- Encourage a clear call to action and benefit for the user.

Injured in an **Accident?**
www.1800needhelp.com/
You May Be Entitled to $10,000 +
Free Case Evaluation. 24/7 Call Us

AdWords ads are made up of the following components:

1. Headline. Your headline has a maximum of 25 characters. With your headline, you should include the keyword the user is searching for, or capture the user's curiosity.

2. Description lines. You have two description lines at a maximum of 35 characters each. Your description lines should make it crystal clear what you are selling, the benefits of clicking through to your site, and a call-to-action, in other words, what you want the user to do.

3. Display URL. You have 35 characters for a custom URL that will be displayed to users in the search results. Display URLs are great as you can actually display a different URL to the users than the URL of the page they will arrive on. You can take advantage of this to encourage more users to arrive on your site.

I've listed below some winning ads so we can see why they are so successful...

Logo Design ® *SALE* $49
www.logodesignguarantee.com/Logo-USA
100% Custom-Made Special USA Sale
100% Money Back. Order Online Now...

Injured in an Accident?
www.1800needhelp.com/
You May Be Entitled to $10,000 +
Free Case Evaluation. 24/7 Call Us

Flowers Online - $19.99
www.fromyouflowers.com/
Delivered Today Beautiful & Fresh!
"Best Value Flowers" - CBS News

In each of the above, we can see some similarities. Each ad has:

- An interesting headline. Each ad captures the curiosity of the user, through use of special characters, asking a question or posting a competitive offer right in the headline.

- Clear benefits. Each ad has a compelling offer making the ad stand out from the search results, such as a no-risk, money-back guarantee, same-day delivery, or a free evaluation.
- A clear call-to-action. The first two ads make it clear what the next step should be. In the third ad, the call-to-action is not explicit, but it is obvious. By having 'Online - $19.99' in the headline, and 'Delivered Today', it is clear the user can order flowers online to be delivered the same-day, if they click on the ad and visit the site.

If you want more examples of successful AdWords ads and why they crush the competition, the article below is a good starting point:

11 successful ads and why they crush the competition
http://blog.crazyegg.com/2012/03/26/successful-adwords-ads/

How much to pay for keywords.

A common burning question for AdWords newbies is... how much should I bid on my keywords?

The Google AdWords cost-per-click network uses a bidding system, which means you are taking place in an auction with competing advertisers. By increasing bids, your ad position increases, leading to more traffic or customers to your site.

Here is where it gets interesting. Google awards an advantage to advertisers showing ads with high quality and high relevancy. This is Google's Quality Score technology. Ads with a higher amount of clicks and relevancy are awarded a higher Quality Score, and receive increased ad positions — at a cheaper price!

Keep this in mind when writing your ads and choosing your keywords. Your ads should be relevant to achieve the highest Quality Score possible, so you can receive the cheapest cost-per-click.

On the other hand, there is no clear answer for predicting your ideal bid price. You should only pay for what you can afford. You can find out how much you can afford by doing some simple math.

For example, lets take the below scenario:

- You're selling video courses for $100.
- For every 100 visitors, 3 turn into customers. This is a conversion rate of 3%.

- If you spend $100 on AdWords, and achieve a $1 cost-per-click, you'll receive $300 in sales, and $200 in profit.

Here's the catch:

You can only find out what your cost-per-click is after running your campaign for a while, when you have accumulated some reliable data. So only run a small test campaign to begin with. Use the information you do have to make some projections, and only pay what you can afford.

Adwords Settings for Getting Started.

The single most important factor in ensuring your campaign is successful is to fill out all of the settings when you set up your campaign. Whatever you do, do not rush through the campaign settings or leave them empty, otherwise you will end up paying for advertising to people who have no interest in what you're selling.

I've listed some recommended AdWords settings below for reference, but if you are not setting up your AdWords campaign right now, feel free to skip to the end of this chapter for some closing recommendations on reviewing AdWords campaigns for long-term success.

1. If you haven't done so already, create an account at http://adwords.google.com. When signing up, enter your Google account, or let the tool create one for you if you don't already have one.

2. Once fully signed in, click on the big button 'Create your first campaign'.

Campaign name:
Enter a descriptive name for your campaign.

Type:
Choose 'search network only' from the drop-down. This is important. Make sure you select this option, unless you know what you are doing, otherwise you will also end up buying advertising on less relevant sites.

Select 'All features - All options for the Search Network, with Display Select'. Why would we want to restrict ourselves and give ourselves less options and features? Choose it, features are juicy. Trust me.

Networks:
Unselect 'include search partners'. We want to advertise on Google, not other smaller, potentially less-relevant sites.

Locations:
If you are targeting customers from a specific area, country, state or city, enter the most relevant setting for your customers here. Whatever you do, don't forget about this setting, otherwise if you're a local business you'll end up buying advertising halfway around the world!

Bid strategy:
Choose 'I'll manually set my bids for clicks'. This allows you to make sure you are only setting cost-per-click bids you can afford. More on setting bids later.

Default bid:
Enter any number here, we are going to change it later.

Budget:
Enter your daily budget.

Ad Extensions:
Ad extensions, otherwise known as sitelinks, are a great way to encourage more clicks to your site. Enter as many relevant entries as you can, if you have an office address and phone number, use it.

Schedule:
If you are only open during certain business hours, enter the hours you want to be running ads here. For some businesses, it's OK to run your campaign 24/7, because some customers will send an online enquiry if they arrive at your site outside of business hours. If you are selling something like a local food, such as a pizza shop, you might want to restrict your campaigns to only run during your opening hours.

Ad delivery:
Choose 'Rotate indefinitely. Show lower performing ads more evenly with higher performing ads, and do not optimize'.

Why would you want to choose this you might wonder? You want to run your ads evenly, so you have reliable data when you review your ads, and can objectively see which ads are performing better for your goals.

You can leave the rest of settings for now, hit 'save and continue', and you're good to go with setting up the rest of your campaign.

Optimization tips for tweaking your campaign for better profit.

I've touched on a handful of secrets of successful pay-per-click campaigns, but I'm going to wrap up this special bonus chapter with the most important habit for pay-per-click success.

Review your campaign regularly.

Leaving an AdWords campaign running without keeping your head around the performance is like leaving a freight train running without a driver.

Regularly review your ad performance, ad group performance, keyword performance, and cost-per-click performance. This will allow you to back the winning horses of your campaign, and swiftly cut the losers.

Fortunately, the AdWords platform offers endless opportunities for deep insights into the performance of your campaign.

As a starting point, below are example areas in your campaign to regularly look over:

- Ad group performance. Review click-through-rates, cost-per-click, and cost-per-conversion. Allocate more funds from your campaign to winning ad groups, and decrease funds or pause losing ad groups if you see any obvious trends.
- Ad performance. Look for winning ads with higher click-through-rates, lower cost-per-clicks, and lower cost-per-conversion. Pause expensive ads, and create new ads to split-test based on your winners. Progressively build up new ads with higher click-through-rates into your campaign over time.
- Keyword performance. Review which keywords are running at a higher cost, which keywords have low quality scores, and see if you can pause any overly budget-draining keywords with low conversions.

That wraps up the special bonus chapter on AdWords.

If you want to delve deeper into the pay-per-click rabbit-hole, the below resources are a great starting point for anyone starting out with pay-per-click advertising:

Ultimate Guide to Google AdWords - Perry Marshall

The ultimate guide to Google Adwords by Perry Marshall is often the starting point for many professionals starting out with PPC. Offers a great overview of AdWords and delves into the 'inner game' of successful AdWords campaigns. Great for beginners, but for advanced techniques check out some of the resources below:

Advanced Google AdWords - Brad Geddes

If you want to be a pay-per-click guru, then look no further than this fantastic guide to advanced AdWords management, for agencies and business owners running their own campaigns. Brad Geddes' magnum opus on advanced AdWords pay-per-click advertising has been the secret treasure of many-a-successful pay-per-click consultant's career. Readily available on Amazon.com

PPC Hero
http://www.ppchero.com

PPC Hero is loaded with free advice on the latest AdWords tricks and tips, but also covering fundamental pay-per-click methods that never change. Updated regularly.

Inside AdWords
http://adwords.blogspot.com

Google's official blog for AdWords. Great for the latest AdWords news direct from the horse's mouth.

Final thoughts.

You could spend decades reading all the different techniques for SEO and never get anywhere. After years of learning what works and what doesn't, I've presented the most effective tactics for SEO and kept this book up-to-date in the face of constant Google changes, to help readers quickly and effectively become skilled at SEO at a professional level.

The advice in this book is more than enough to get started in SEO and increase rankings, traffic and sales for your site.

But don't forget why we learn SEO in the first place.

The details are important, but don't get bogged down in them. It's painfully easy to get lost in the endless sea of information on SEO and never make any progress with your projects or goals.

What matters is you optimize your site well enough to beat your competitors, make more sales, and grow your business.

These strategies work for my projects, they work for my clients and they will work for you. If your site shows stronger signals to Google than your competitors, you will beat them in the rankings.

Most importantly, have fun with it.

~

Corrections, suggestions & complaints — please do this:

If you are unhappy with this book for any reason, noticed a mistake, or want something included, give me a chance to fix it and email me at adamclarkeseobook@gmail.com. I want this book to be the best for all readers, which is why feedback is important. I use feedback in future updates as much as possible.

What's next.

If you would like me to write more books on growing your business, in this simple and easy to understand format, please take a moment, support this book and put up some stars and a review on Amazon. It will make my day. Thank you.

- Adam Clarke

http://bit.ly/seo-2016-book